Labour and Employment Compliance in Belgium

D1719189

International Bar Association

Labour and Employment Compliance
in Belgium

Seventh Edition

Chris Van Olmen

This publication is part of the International Labour
and Employment Compliance Handbook,
available on www.kluwerlawonline.com

Editors: Salvador del Rey and Robert J. Mignin
Associate Editor: Juan Bonilla

the global voice of
the legal profession

Published by:
Kluwer Law International B.V.
PO Box 316
2400 AH Alphen aan den Rijn
The Netherlands
E-mail: lrs-sales@wolterskluwer.com
Website: www.wolterskluwer.com/en/solutions/kluwerlawinternational

Sold and distributed by:
Wolters Kluwer Legal & Regulatory U.S.
7201 McKinney Circle
Frederick, MD 21704
United States of America
E-mail: customer.service@wolterskluwer.com

Printed on acid-free paper.

ISBN 978-94-035-4374-1

e-Book: ISBN 978-94-035-4704-6
web-PDF: ISBN 978-94-035-4714-5

© 2022 Kluwer Law International BV, The Netherlands

Printed in the United Kingdom.

All listed titles are also available on lrus.wolterskluwer.com

1. Argentina: Julio César Stefanoni Zani & Enrique Alfredo Betemps, *Labour and Employment Compliance in Argentina, 10th edition*, 2022 (ISBN 978-94-035-4332-1)
2. Australia: John Tuck, Stephen Price, Rosemary Roach, Jack de Flamingh, Nicholas Ellery & Nick Le Mare, *Labour and Employment Compliance in Australia, 6th edition*, 2021 (ISBN 978-94-035-3914-0)
3. Belgium: Chris Van Olmen, *Labour and Employment Compliance in Belgium, 7th edition*, 2022 (ISBN 978-94-035-4374-1)
4. Brazil: Rodrigo Seizo Takano, Andrea Giamondo Massei & Murilo Caldeira Germiniani, *Labour and Employment Compliance in Brazil, 9th edition*, 2022 (ISBN 978-94-035-4991-0)
5. Canada: Kevin Coon & Adrian Ishak, *Labour and Employment Compliance in Canada, 2nd edition*, 2014 (ISBN 978-90-411-5637-2)
6. Chile: Gerardo Otero A., María Dolores Echeverría F., María de los Ángeles Fernández S. & Javier Sabido, *Labour and Employment Compliance in Chile, 9th edition*, 2021 (ISBN 978-94-035-3635-4)
7. China: King & Wood Mallesons, *Labour and Employment Compliance in China, 6th edition*, 2021 (ISBN 978-94-035-3894-5)
8. France: Pascale Lagesse, *Labour and Employment Compliance in France, 9th edition*, 2021 (ISBN 978-94-035-3672-9)
9. Germany: Gerlind Wisskirchen & Martin Lützeler, *Labour and Employment Compliance in Germany, 9th edition*, 2021 (ISBN 978-94-035-3605-7)
10. India: Manishi Pathak, *Labour and Employment Compliance in India, 10th edition*, 2022 (ISBN 978-94-035-4362-8)
11. Ireland: Duncan Inverarity & Ailbhe Dennehy, *Labour and Employment Compliance in Ireland, 8th edition*, 2021 (ISBN 978-94-035-3911-9)
12. Israel: Pnina Broder-Manor, Helen Raziel & Ilan Winder, *Labour and Employment Compliance in Israel, 8th edition*, 2021 (ISBN 978-94-035-3612-5)
13. Italy: Angelo Zambelli, *Labour and Employment Compliance in Italy, 10th edition*, 2022 (ISBN 978-94-035-4372-7)
14. Japan: Yoshikazu Sugino, *Labour and Employment Compliance in Japan, 10th edition*, 2022 (ISBN 978-94-035-4342-0)
15. Republic of Korea: Sang Wook Cho, Soojung Lee & Christopher Mandel, *Labour and Employment Compliance in the Republic of Korea, 7th edition*, 2021 (ISBN 978-94-035-3645-3)
16. Mexico: Oscar De La Vega Gómez, *Labour and Employment Compliance in Mexico, 9th edition*, 2021 (ISBN 978-94-035-3615-6)
17. The Netherlands: Els de Wind & Cara Pronk, *Labour and Employment Compliance in the Netherlands, 5th edition*, 2022 (ISBN 978-94-035-1594-6)
18. Poland: Barbara Jóźwik, *Labour and Employment Compliance in Poland, 9th edition*, 2021 (ISBN 978-94-035-3675-0)
19. Russia: Anna-Stefaniya Chepik, *Labour and Employment Compliance in Russia*, 2013 (ISBN 978-90-411-4925-1)

20. Saudi Arabia: Sara Khoja & Sarit Thomas, *Labour and Employment Compliance in Saudi Arabia, 4th edition,* 2021 (ISBN 978-94-035-3652-1)
21. South Africa: Susan Stelzner, Stuart Harrison, Brian Patterson & Zahida Ebrahim, *Labour and Employment Compliance in South Africa, 9th edition,* 2021 (ISBN 978-94-035-2773-4)
22. Spain: Salvador del Rey, Ana Campos & Sergi Gálvez Duran, *Labour and Employment Compliance in Spain, 10th edition,* 2022 (978-94-035-4352-9)
23. Turkey: Sertaç Kökenek & Elif Nur Çakır Vurgun, *Labour and Employment Compliance in Turkey, 7th edition,* 2021 (ISBN 978-94-035-3901-0)
24. United Arab Emirates: Sara Khoja & Sarit Thomas, *Labour and Employment Compliance in the United Arab Emirates, 8th edition,* 2021 (ISBN 978-94-035-3655-2)
25. United Kingdom: Ed Mills, Ailie Murray, Anna West, Gareth Walls, Emmie Ellison & Elliot English, *Labour and Employment Compliance in The United Kingdom, 2nd edition,* 2021 (ISBN 978-94-035-3904-1)
26. United States: Andrew J. Boling, Amy de La Lama, William Dugan, Chris Guldberg, Brian Hengesbaugh, Robert J. Mignin, Virginia Mohr, John M. Murphy & Ginger Partee, *Labour and Employment Compliance in the United States, 7th edition,* 2022 (ISBN 978-94-035-3921-8)

International Bar Association
The Global Voice of the Legal Profession

The International Bar Association (IBA), established in 1947, is the world's leading organization of international legal practitioners, bar associations and law societies. The IBA influences the development of international law reform and shapes the future of the legal profession throughout the world. It has a membership of over 40,000 individual lawyers and almost 200 bar associations and law societies spanning all continents. It has considerable expertise in providing assistance to the global legal community.

Grouped into two divisions – the Legal Practice Division and the Public and Professional Interest Division – the IBA covers all practice areas and professional interests, providing members with access to leading experts and up-to-date information. Through the various committees of the divisions, the IBA enables an interchange of information and views among its members as to laws, practices and professional responsibilities relating to the practice of business law around the globe. Additionally, the IBA's high-quality publications and world-class conferences provide unrivalled professional development and network-building opportunities for international legal practitioners and professional associates.

The IBA's Bar Issues Commission provides an invaluable forum for IBA member organisations to discuss all matters relating to law at an international level.

The IBA's Human Rights Institute (IBAHRI) works across the Association, to promote, protect and enforce human rights under a just rule of law, and to preserve the independence of the judiciary and the legal profession worldwide.

Other institutions established by the IBA include the Southern Africa Litigation Centre and the International Legal Assistance Consortium.

Employment and Industrial Relations Law Committee

The aims of the committee are to develop and exchange knowledge of employment and industrial relations law and practice. Members support each other through the provision of innovative ideas and practical assistance on day-to-day issues. In addition, through its journal and through presentations, conferences, the committee ensures the dissemination of up-to-date law and practice in this highly important business area.

International Bar Association Global Employment Institute

The IBA Global Employment Institute (IBA GEI) was formed in early 2010 for the purpose of developing for multinationals and worldwide institutions a global and strategic approach to the key legal issues in the human resources and human capital fields.

Drawing on the resources and expertise of the IBA membership, the IBA GEI will provide a unique contribution in the field of employment, discrimination and immigration law, on a diverse range of global issues, to private and public organizations throughout the world. The IBA GEI is designed to enhance the management, performance and productivity of these organizations and help achieve best practice in their human capital and management functions from a strategic perspective.

The IBA GEI will become the leading voice and authority on global HR issues by virtue of having a number of the world's leading labour and employment practitioners in its ranks, and the support and resource of the world's largest association of international lawyers.

Further information

International Bar Association, 4th Floor, 10 St Bride Street, London EC4A 4AD, United Kingdom, Tel: +44 (0)20 7842 0090, Fax: +44 (0)20 7842 0091, E-mail: member@int-bar.org, www.ibanet.org

About the International Labour and Employment Compliance Handbook

From 1976 through 1988, the International Bar Association and Kluwer Law International published the groundbreaking International Handbook on Contracts of Employment. This Handbook provided one of the first global overviews of the law of the international employment relationship.

Since publishing the first edition, globalization of business has created an increased demand for knowledge of labor and employment laws throughout the world. Therefore, along with Kluwer, we decided to publish an updated Handbook which we have titled the International Labour and Employment Compliance Handbook.

This new Handbook was intended to be a practical guide by providing a general overview of key labor and employment issues in multiple jurisdictions. Each chapter was written so that it is easy to understand by lawyers and non-lawyers alike. Each country author has also followed a standard outline to assist readers in analysing employment issues in each country.

The first edition of this new Handbook included nineteen (19) different countries.

This Handbook would not have been possible without the help and assistance of many people. Most importantly, the individual country authors are all distinguished legal practitioners who spent considerable time drafting and revising their country reports to meet difficult deadlines. We thank each of them. Our friends at Kluwer, especially Ewa Szkatula, have done a wonderful job in keeping the editors and the authors on schedule. Finally, we want to also express our gratitude to Cuatrecasas, Gonçalves Pereira, and Baker & McKenzie LLP for their valuable assistance in the coordination and organization of this project. Our warmest thanks to each of them.

Because of the success of the Handbook, Wolters Kluwer Law & Business decided to publish each country report also as a separate book to give a choice in obtaining the information. We hope this new format will be a helpful and useful resource just like the Handbook. Both formats are available in print and online.

The Editors

Salvador del Rey Guanter
Robert J. Mignin

March 2013

Table of Contents

Belgium

AUTHOR

Chris Van Olmen

Chris Van Olmen is the founding partner of the law firm Van Olmen & Wynant, a 'boutique' law firm focusing on employment law, and he is Chairman of L&E Global, an integrated alliance of premier employment law boutique firms (www.leglobal.org).

Since 1999, he has been lecturing on Social Law in the traineeship programme organized by the Brussels Bar. He also served as a member of the Brussels Bar Council and is a board member of the Association for Social Law.

Chris Van Olmen is the Co-Chair of the Global Employment Institute and former Co-Chair of the Employment and Industrial Relations Law Committee of the IBA (International Bar Association).

Chris is also a member of the European Employment Lawyers Association and the American Bar Association (labour and employment law section) and has been a speaker or moderator at numerous national and international seminars and conferences.

ADDRESS

Van Olmen & Wynant
Avenue Louise 221
1050 Brussels
Belgium
Tel.: +32 2 644 05 11
Fax: +32 2 646 38 47
E-mail: chris.van.olmen@vow.be
Web: http://www.vow.be

BELGIUM

Legal Compliance in Belgium

1. THE LEGAL FRAMEWORK

1.1. OVERVIEW OF THE DIFFERENT SOURCES OF LAW

Belgian employment law is based on both international and national sources. The former comprises of international treaties and conventions, such as the United Nations Treaties and conventions of the International Labour Organization. European law, as laid down in the European Union (EU) Treaties, as well as in Regulations, Directives or Decisions, also regulates various matters related to labour and employment within the EU. Case law of the European Court of Justice (ECJ), such as its preliminary rulings on the exact interpretation of EU law, helps elucidate these rules and is another prominent source of Belgian employment law. Also, the treaties of the Council of Europe – The European Convention of Human Rights and the European Social Charter (the revised version of 1996) – have been ratified by Belgium. The case law of the European Court of Human Rights and, to a lesser degree, the conclusions and decisions of the European Committee for Social Rights have an impact on the Belgian legal order.

The national sources of employment law in Belgium are, first and foremost, the Belgian Constitution and numerous federal laws, in particular, the Act of 3 July 1978 on Employment Contracts (Employment Contracts Act). Royal and Ministerial Decrees further implement these laws. Since Belgium became a federal state, its Regions[1] and Communities[2] have become competent to regulate certain matters that touch upon issues that are

---

1. Flemish (Dutch-speaking), Walloon (French-speaking) and Brussels region (bilingual) – the Regions' competencies are mostly related to economic matters.
2. Flemish, French-speaking and German Communities – the Communities are mainly concerned with cultural matters. However, it should be noted that in Flanders, the Region and Community have become one, whereas for the French-speaking part of the country, the French-speaking Community should be distinguished from the Brussels and Walloon Regions.

related to labour and employment (e.g., regional re-employment services and the use of language in the work environment). Collective bargaining between the so-called Social Partners (Trade Unions and Employers' Organizations) also plays a major role in shaping the rules of employment law. Collective Bargaining Agreements (CBAs) are entered into at a national or an industry level by representatives of both organizations or at a company level between the employer and Union representatives.

At the heart of every working relationship lies an individual agreement between an employee and his/her employer. More often than not, both parties will detail the conditions that they agreed upon in a written employment contract. Complementary to this source of law is the so-called Work Rules (*arbeidsreglement* – *règlement du travail*), i.e., a document containing a set of rules that are proper to the employer and the employees of the undertaking and that every employer must establish. Finally, customary law, often specific to certain industries, may also apply.

Following the civil law tradition, case law precedents have, in principle, no legally binding force in Belgium.[3] However, decisions rendered by the highest courts – the Supreme Court (*Hof van Cassatie* – *Cour de cassation*) or the Constitutional Court (*Grondwettelijk Hof* – *Cour constitutionnelle*) – have strong persuasive authority and will generally be followed by the Labour Tribunals and Labour Courts of Appeal.

With so many rules deriving from various sources, conflicts between them inevitably emerge, which calls for a set of rules to determine which rules will prevail. International law will prevail over national law whenever the former is directly applicable. Inconsistencies between national sources of law are to be resolved following Article 51 of the Collective Labour Agreements and Joint Committees[4] Act of 5 December 1968. Binding provisions of the law are at the top of this hierarchical classification, while custom is at the bottom. Written individual employment contracts will prevail over the Work Rules but must comply with binding CBAs, whether entered into on a national, industry or company level.

---

3. However, if the Supreme Court is asked for the second time to render a decision on the same question of law in the same case, its decision will be binding for the court that the case will be referred to.
4. A Joint Committee is a body established per sector of industry in which the Unions and the employers' organizations are represented. Within these Joint Committees, CBAs are entered into, which include terms governing minimum wages and other employment conditions. Three types of Joint Committees exist: Joint Committees that are only competent for white-collar employees, Joint Committees that are only competent for blue-collar employees and mixed Joint Committees that are competent for both blue- and white-collar employees.

1.2. THE EMPLOYMENT CONTRACTS ACT AND OTHER LABOUR LAWS IN BELGIUM

Apart from the Employment Contracts Act, the major Acts which govern employment and labour law in Belgium are the Labour Act of 1971 on working time and conditions, the Employment Relations Act of 2006 and the Acts with regard to discrimination and well-being.

The Employment Contracts Act sets out the major principles regarding employment contracts. Its original *summa divisio* between blue-collar employees and white-collar employees, considered discriminatory by the Belgian Constitutional Court, was abandoned. Since the commencement of the Unified Employment Status Act on 1 January 2014, the same notice periods apply for both categories of employees, and the unpaid 'waiting day'[5] (*carensdag – jour de carence*) for blue-collar employees was suppressed. However, some differences between both categories of employees in other fields of the employment relationship remain and still need to be adjusted during a second phase of the harmonization process (*see* section 2.1).

The Labour Act of 16 March 1971 aims to strike a balance between the need to protect employees, and especially their right not to find themselves at their employer's beck and call at all times, and the need for employers to ensure they can maintain their competitive position. To that end, this Act defines normal working hours and explicitly prohibits working at night, on Sundays, on Public Holidays or beyond a fixed, part-time schedule, with the exception of well-defined situations as set out in the Act.

The 2006 Employment Relations Act defines and outlines the exact notion of the employment contract, as opposed to a working relationship between independent contractors. It aims to prevent contracting parties from depriving employees of the labour and social security protections they are entitled to by entering into self-employed contracts, which hide the true nature of the working relationship. Parties are entitled to choose the basis on which they wish to cooperate (self-employed or employed). This choice will be upheld by Labour Courts and social security authorities, provided there are no facts relating to the performance of work that contradict the contractual characterization of the working relationship.

The General Act of 10 May 2007 prohibits discrimination on the basis of age, sexual preference, civil status, birth, wealth, belief or personal convictions, political convictions, language, current or future health conditions, handicap, physical or genetic characteristics or social background. The second Act of 10 May 2007 prohibits discrimination between men and women. Finally, the Act of 30 July 1981 prohibits

---

5. Contrary to white-collar employees, blue-collar employees did not receive their normal wages on the first day of illness. This was deemed discriminatory.

discrimination on the basis of nationality, so-called race, the colour of skin, background or national or ethnic origin. These Acts, as well as the constitutional rights of equal treatment and the right not to be discriminated against,[6] also permeate the working environment in all its aspects, including access to work and working conditions during the employment relationship or at the time of termination, both in the private and public sectors.

The Act of 1996 on the well-being of workers establishes the framework for the health and safety obligations at the workplace. The detailed rules for the execution of the principles of the Act of 1996 are laid down in the Well-Being Codex. Next to all kinds of prevention obligations, employers are also required to protect their employees from all 'psychosocial risks', a notion that will call for action on its behalf, even without an employee having to prove a specific act of violence, bullying or sexual harassment. The Well-Being Act and Codex also set out specific procedures on how to intervene when employees are confronted with these problems, as well as regarding the risk analysis the employer must conduct on work-related stress in its company.

1.3.   Decisions Rendered by the Belgian Labour Courts

The Belgian Labour Tribunals (First Instance) and Labour Courts of Appeal are independent judicial bodies whose jurisdiction covers all matters related to labour and social security law. Against decisions rendered by the Labour Courts of Appeal, only appeals on matters of law can be lodged with the Supreme Court. A professional judge presides over the Labour Courts, assisted by two lay judges, one a representative from the employers' side and the other from the employees' side. Plaintiffs may bring their case to court in person or by legal representation, either by an attorney (*advocaat – avocat*) or by a member of their Trade Union acting by special proxy. Enforcement of labour law provisions may also be initiated by administrative authorities, such as the Social Inspectorate or tax and social security authorities.

Many rules of Belgian labour law are enforced by criminal punishment. Failure to abide by the rules may thus give rise to criminal sanctions imposed on the corporation as well as its directors.[7]

---

6. Articles 10–11 of the Constitution.
7. As laid down by the Social Penal Code, *see* s. 13.8.

2. CONTRACTS OF EMPLOYMENT

2.1. OVERVIEW

An employment contract is an agreement in the frame of which an employee receives remuneration in return for the carrying out of work under the authority of an employer.

It is this last element, namely the right of the employer to exert authority, that distinguishes an employment contract from a self-employed working relationship. If a link of subordination exists between the parties, the employment relationship is deemed to be an employment contract. If not, the relationship will be considered as a working relationship on a self-employed basis (*see* section 8.2).

Although a standard practice, there is no obligation for an employer to enter into a written employment contract. The employment agreement may also be entered into verbally (*see* section 2.2: enumeration of certain types of contracts and clauses which must be in writing).

In principle, the parties are free to fix the terms of their employment contract. However, the mandatory legal and regulatory conditions (in particular the Employment Contracts Act of 3 July 1978), as well as the conditions within CBAs, are generally deemed to form an integral part of the employment contract, and no clause may validly depart from these conditions. If so, such clauses are null and void and cannot be invoked against the employee. Therefore, in practice, the parties' freedom to establish the terms of employment by mutual agreement is strictly circumscribed by law.

The agreed conditions, or stipulations, of an employment contract cannot be changed unilaterally. An employee could claim damages in case of unilateral modification of his/her remuneration or working conditions. If the modification is substantial, the contract could even be regarded as being terminated by the employer (constructive dismissal). However, parties can specify – to a certain extent – that the employer has the right to unilaterally modify elements expressly qualified as an accessory.

The open-ended employment contract is the most common employment contract used in Belgium. If not explicitly stipulated otherwise, every employment contract is presumed to be for an indefinite term.

Yet, other types of employment contracts exist and can broadly be subdivided on the basis of: (i) the period for which the contract is entered into; (ii) the volume of work performed (full-time versus part-time contracts); and (iii) the nature of the work performed.

The most important consideration is the distinction based on the period for which the employment contract is entered into (i.e., open-ended employment contracts and fixed-term employment contracts).

A fixed-term contract automatically ends upon the expiry date of the contract. Yet, if parties continue to perform the contract after its expiry date, the employment contract will be deemed to be an open-ended employment contract.

The Employment Contracts Act limits the ability of parties entering into multiple consecutive fixed-term employment contracts (in general, a maximum of four consecutive contracts of a minimum of three months and for a total duration of a maximum of two years is set, or – with the prior permission of the Labour Inspectorate – consecutive contracts of a minimum of six months and for a total duration of three years may be entered into). In cases of violations of this restriction, consecutive fixed-term employment contracts are considered to be for an indefinite term (unless the employer proves that these contracts were justified because of the nature of the job or because of another legitimate reason).

An employment contract for a specific project or a replacement contract is also a type of fixed-term contract.

The employment contract for a specific project will end on the date on which the project is completed, even though no specific time can be set.

A replacement contract may be entered into to replace an employee whose employment contract has been suspended for reasons other than lack of work for economic reasons, the weather, a strike, or lockout (for instance, long-time illness, pregnancy or maternity leave, or a career break). The duration of such a contract may not exceed two years (except in the framework of a career break) and generally ends upon the return of the replaced employee.

A further type of employment contract is an employment contract for the performance of temporary work. Such contracts are used to address a temporary lack of personnel, replace a permanent employee, manage a temporary increase in workload, or carry out an exceptional task.

The Employment Contracts Act also distinguishes on the basis of the nature of the work performed, i.e., between an employment contract for white-collar employees, blue-collar employees, sales representatives and domestic servants.

The distinction between blue- and white-collar employees evolved historically but is outdated and discriminatory, according to the Belgian Constitutional Court. A first step towards the harmonization of the employment status of blue- and white-collar employees was taken with the Unified Employment Status Act, which came into force on 1 January 2014. It lifted the distinction between both categories of employees with regard to notice periods, the trial period (which was abolished), and the unpaid 'waiting day' (*carensdag – jour de carence*) for blue-collar employees (first day of illness), which was suppressed. Yet, to date, the differences in other fields still need to be adjusted during the second phase of this harmonization process (e.g., the holiday rules, occupational pension plans, and merging the separate Joint Committees for blue- and white-collar employees).

The employment contract for a sales representative can be similar to an employment contract for an ordinary white-collar employee, except for a non-competition clause, which is different for a sales representative. Yet, as this type of employee delivers very specific services, employment contracts for sales representatives often include specific clauses with regard to wages (fixed salary and/or commissions) and a 'del credere clause' (liability of the sales representative for the customer's creditworthiness).

The employment contract for domestic servants is to be entered into for housekeeping work at the home of the employer. It is, however, not frequently used.

Stipulations that are often included within a written employment contract are: the date of entering into service, the function for which the employee is hired, the remuneration of the employee, a confidentiality clause, and a non-competition clause.

Although it is recommended, in principle, there is no obligation to list the benefits in the employment contract as they can also be documented separately. An exception to this rule relates to any arrangement with regard to remuneration and costs linked to homework/structural telework, which must be included within the employment contract or an annex thereto.

The standard employment contract is the one entered into between one employer and one employee. Yet, if two legal entities both exercise (part of) the employer's authority and are closely linked – in general, companies pertaining to the same international group or a mother-daughter company – the employment contract can be entered into with two employers.

A more recent option is the so-called employers' association (*werkgeversgroepering – groupement d'employeurs*). In the frame of such an 'employers' association', two or more companies can jointly hire (an) employee(s) who will work for the different members of the association. The employee enters into one single employment contract with the association that puts the employee at the disposal of its different members. The different members will be jointly liable for all payments to the employee (wages, etc.) or a third party (the social security office, tax authorities, etc.). The employers' association needs to comply with certain legal formalities and must be approved beforehand by the Minister of Work. Due to the complexity of the rules, this option is still not popular in Belgium.

2.2. WRITTEN EMPLOYMENT CONTRACTS

In principle, the standard employment contract, namely the full-time, open-ended employment contract, may be written or verbal. Yet, for all other employment contracts deviating from this standard, the Belgian Employment Contracts Act requires a written document. This is, for instance, the case for:

- employment contracts for a fixed term;
- employment contracts for a specific project;
- employment contracts for part-time work;
- replacement contracts;
- employment contracts for domestic servants;
- employment contracts for students;
- employment contracts for temporary agency work;
- employment contracts for structural telework;
- employment contracts for homework.

Most of these contracts must be signed before the employee actually starts his/her activity. In case of an employment contract for a fixed term, a specific project, a replacement contract or a contract for temporary work, the sanction in case of absence of a written contract entered into before the employment commences will be that the agreement will be considered to be for an indefinite term.

A number of employment contracts that need to be laid down in writing also need to include a number of predetermined stipulations. For instance, this is the case for a replacement contract (must indicate the reason for the replacement, the identity of the replaced employee,[8] etc.), a contract for students (must include a whole set of compulsory stipulations, among which the starting and ending date of the agreement, the place of work, the working time per day and per week, etc.), homeworkers (must indicate the place chosen by the homeworker to do his/her job, a brief description of the work agreed upon, the competent Joint Committee, etc.).

If no document was made, or if the contract does not include these obligatory statements, the employee can terminate the contract without observing a notice period or paying an indemnity in lieu.

An employment contract for part-time work must include the employee's fixed work schedule (or a reference to the variable work schedules contained in the Work Rules) and work arrangements. In the absence thereof, the employee may choose the work schedule and work arrangements that are most favourable to him/her among those included within the Work Rules[9] or in any other company document (which are apparent from a social record which the employer is obliged to keep).

Also, certain clauses, such as a non-competition clause, an arbitral clause for high-paid employees with high management responsibilities, and a

---

8. However, a replacement contract can also be used in case the company faces a high rate of absenteeism.

9. *See* s. 2.4. hereinafter for a definition of Work Rules.

training clause (*scholingsbeding – clause d'écolage*), need to be laid down in writing. These clauses are not obligatory, but if they are entered into, they need to comply with formal requirements. If not, they will be null and void.

The Unified Employment Status Act abolished the trial period for contracts taking effect as of 1 January 2014. Therefore, it is no longer possible to include a trial period in an employment contract. However, as a way to reintroduce some kind of trial period, shorter notice periods have been prescribed in case of dismissal by the employer during the first six months of employment. Also, an exception exists for student contracts, temporary work, and temporary agency work. For these contracts, the trial period (first three days of the contract) automatically applies and therefore does not need to be inserted into the written employment contract.

For some employment contracts (e.g., the employment contract of each part-time employee), the employer needs to keep a copy at the place where the Work Rules can be consulted. For other contracts, such as an employment contract for students, a copy must be sent to the Labour Inspectorate.

A characteristic of employment contracts[10] in Belgium is that, when in written form, they must be drafted in French, Dutch or German, depending on the location of the employer's operating unit. For instance, if the operating unit to which the employee is attached and where the social relations between parties occur is located in the Flemish region, the employment contract must be drafted in Dutch. If the operating unit is in the Walloon region, the employment contract must be drafted in French, and if the location is in the German-speaking region, the contract must be in German. For the Brussels region, the employment contract must be either in French or Dutch, depending on the language used by the employee.

Yet, in a judgment of 16 April 2013 (Case C-202/11), the ECJ has ruled that EU law must be interpreted as precluding legislation of a federated entity of a Member State, such as that applicable in Flanders, which requires all employers whose established place of business is located in that entity's territory to draft cross-border employment contracts exclusively in the official language of that federated entity, failing which the contracts are to be declared null and void by the national courts of their own motion.

The Flemish Decree on the use of languages in social relations has been modified with a view to ensuring compliance with that ruling. It now provides that a version having legal force may be established for employment contracts in one of the languages of the EU understood by all the parties concerned in cases where the employee may claim free movement rights on the basis of EU law or of any other international or

---

10. And all employment-related documents between the employer and the employee for that matter.

supranational treaty. In case of conflict with the Flemish version, the Flemish version of the contract will prevail.

Although the case before the Court of Justice of the European Union (CJEU) only referred to employment contracts and the Flemish Decree now only allows the existence of a translation, the majority of the Belgian case law seems to allow the use of English in all social relations whenever the employer can prove that the company and/or the employee operate in an international context. However, the discussion is far from over and the Belgian legislation on the use of languages is still quite strict.

Most employment contracts in Belgium are signed manually (handwritten) by the employer and the employee. Yet, an employment contract can also be signed electronically with a qualified electronic signature,[11] compliant to EU Regulation No 910/2014 (eIDAS Regulation), if both parties agree to this. A copy of the electronically signed employment contract must then be stored with a provider of electronic archiving services.

2.3. ORAL CONTRACTS

As indicated, a full-time, open-ended employment contract may be written or verbal. Yet, to avoid any difficulties of proof if a conflict arises, it is prudent and advisable to enter into a written contract.

If an employment contract is not in writing, it is always deemed to have been entered into for an indefinite term.

If an employment contract is in writing, it can still be replaced or amended verbally. For instance, an employment contract for part-time work, which needs to be entered into in writing, can be modified verbally into a full-time employment contract.

2.4. EMPLOYEE HANDBOOKS

In Belgium, a distinction should be made between the 'Work Rules', which constitute a mandatory document, and 'internal policies', which are useful but not mandatory.

The Work Rules (*arbeidsreglement – règlement de travail*) include a set of rules that are proper and applicable to the employer and the employee(s) of its undertaking. This document is mandatory for each employer (Belgian or foreign) employing (an) employee(s) in Belgium. The employer's failure to adhere to the obligation to adopt Work Rules is a penal act.

---

11. A qualified electronic signature is an advanced electronic signature with a qualified digital certificate that has been created by a qualified signature creation device. This enables to verify the authorship of a signature in electronic data exchange over long periods of time.

The Work Rules must include a number of compulsory provisions and procedures (e.g., working time schedules, measurement and control of the work done, the duties and rights of the supervisory personnel, disciplinary measures and sanctions, a declaration of intent and/or policy with regard to alcohol and drugs, and a procedure with regard to psychosocial risks at work, including sexual harassment and mobbing). A number of optional provisions agreed upon between employer and employee(s) may be added hereto. The Work Rules must be drafted in the correct language, i.e., French, Dutch or German, depending on the location of the employer's operating unit (*see* section 2.2 in this respect).

For the adoption or amendment of the Work Rules, a specific procedure needs to be followed (the Work Rules are to be adopted by the Works Council, or in the absence thereof, the employees are allowed to make comments on a draft posted by the employer).

Work Rules are only binding on individual employees when they have received a copy from their employer, even if they were informed through different channels.

Other internal policies are not mandatory but could be useful to make clear arrangements on specific topics. The following policies are often adopted by Belgian employers:

– a car policy;
– a mobility policy;
– a Code of Conduct;
– a policy on the use of e-mail, Internet and social media;
– a policy with regard to the use of a mobile phone, laptop, tablet;
– a policy on the reimbursement of costs;
– a 'bring your own device' policy;
– a General Data Protection Regulation (GDPR) policy;
– a telework policy.

They should also be drafted or translated into the correct language.

2.5. JOB DESCRIPTIONS

Job descriptions detail the employee's main tasks and assignments. They may not include any discriminatory provisions.

It is not an obligation for employers to draw up a detailed job description; however, a good job description can be an important tool with regard to HR management as it sets clear job expectations and helps with regard to promotion and compensation.

CBAs entered into within a Joint Committee generally include a list of functions and/or a (brief) job description, which are classified into different categories. For each of these categories, a minimum wage is set (*see also* section 10.1).

The function, job content, and nature of the responsibilities of the employee are considered to be an essential element of the employment contract, along with the employee's wage, place of work, and hours of work.

Any unilateral and substantial change of such function or job content can therefore be regarded as a breach of contract and runs the risk of being qualified as a constructive dismissal, allowing the employee to claim an indemnity in lieu of notice.

2.6. OFFER LETTERS

An offer for employment is an expression of willingness to enter into an employment contract on certain terms, made with the intention that it shall become binding as soon as it is accepted by the candidate.

An offer for employment exists when the simple acceptance of a proposition of the employer by the candidate results in the constitution of an employment contract. Therefore, mere negotiations or preliminary discussions do not constitute a job offer.

The employer may revoke an offer, but only before it has been accepted. Once accepted, the contract becomes final, and the signing of a formal employment contract is not necessary.

2.7. CHECKLIST OF DOS AND DON'TS

- For employment contracts deviating from the standard full-time, open-ended employment contract, it is obligatory to draw up a written document. Yet, also for the standard full-time, open-ended employment contract, it is highly recommended to provide for a written contract to avoid any difficulties of proof and to avoid conflicts.
- When entering into consecutive fixed-term employment contracts, check beforehand if such succession of contracts is allowed.
- For sales representatives, it can be advisable to include specific clauses within the employment contract (a 'del credere clause', a specific non-competition clause, a clause with regard to commissions, etc.).
- Keep in mind that a number of employment contracts (such as a replacement contract, a contract for students, and a contract for homeworkers) must include a number of predetermined stipulations.
- Verify if all employment contracts for part-time work include the fixed work schedule (or a reference to the variable work schedules contained in the Work Rules) and work arrangements of the employee.

- It is very important that employment contracts, as well as any other employment documents for that matter, are drafted in the correct language (French, Dutch, or German, depending on the location of the employer's operating unit). Documents in violation of the language regulations applicable within the Dutch and French language region are null and void, and the lifting of this nullity by a replacement document will only have an effect going forward. However, for the German-speaking region and employers having their operating unit in the bilingual area of Brussels, documents drafted in the wrong language can be replaced, and the replacement document will take effect retroactively.
- Check if a set of Work Rules has been drafted, correctly implemented and whether they include all obligatory provisions and are up-to-date.
- It is advisable to draw up specific policies, such as a car policy, a policy on the use of e-mail, Internet and social media, and a mobile phone and laptop policy.
- Check the CBAs entered into at an industry level as they include the minimum wages and working conditions that will be applicable.

3. RECRUITING, INTERVIEWING, SCREENING AND HIRING EMPLOYEES

3.1. OVERVIEW

The principles of recruiting are laid down in CBA No. 38 on the recruitment and selection of employees. Employers are forbidden from asking certain questions of applicants or requiring them to undergo certain tests. The purpose of background checks must be to assess the applicant's ability to fulfil the job. Questions and tests that violate the applicant's privacy rights or are discriminatory are prohibited by the data privacy legislation (i.e., Regulation (EU) 2016/679 of the European Parliament and of the Council of 27 April 2016 on the protection of natural persons with regard to the processing of personal data and on the free movement of such data – hereinafter referred to as 'GDPR' – and the Act of 30 July 2018 on the protection of natural persons with regard to the processing of data, which entered into force on 5 September 2018), anti-discrimination legislation (Acts of 10 May 2007 and 7 July 1981 prohibiting discrimination on the grounds of, among others, age, gender, sexual orientation, marital status, birth, wealth, religious or philosophical beliefs, political convictions, language, state of health, handicap, nationality, supposed race, colour, and ancestry ethnic origin) and by a CBA covering all employers and employees in the private sector (CBA No. 38 of 6 December 1983 on the recruitment and selection of employees).

3.2.   RECRUITING

In principle, an employer should supply applicants with sufficient information about the vacancy. Job offers should contain at least a job description, the skills required to perform the function, and the location of the workplace.

As a rule, an employer can only ask questions to an applicant that are genuinely relevant, taking into consideration the nature and working conditions of the job offered (such as diplomas and previous jobs).

The applicant has the right not to answer questions that are not relevant to the job or violate privacy and anti-discrimination laws. However, it is worth noting that applicants have an obligation to cooperate in good faith during the selection process. An applicant is not only bound to answer the employer's relevant questions but should also spontaneously provide the employer with all relevant information that he/she might be expected to know and which would be important to the employer. In case an applicant provides false information, the employment contract could be terminated for serious cause based on error or deceit. However, this is only the case when the false information is relevant to the application procedure (e.g., the applicant does not have the required diplomas or hides medical information that could endanger himself or a co-worker).

3.3.   EMPLOYMENT APPLICATIONS

The applicant's individual file has to be protected from third-party access and treated confidentially. In addition, an employer may collect data only from the applicant and not from third parties. When reverting to third parties to collect personal data, the employer must obtain prior consent from the applicant.

An employer is not allowed to oblige the applicant to present sealed and certified copies of diplomas, certificates, or other documents but should be satisfied with a decent copy. However, in case of doubt with regard to the veracity of the documents, the employer can ask to see the original, or they could verify the authenticity with the Institution who granted the document (e.g., a university). In compliance with the GDPR, such an Institution will only help with the verification if they receive the consent of the data subject (the candidate).

The information included within an employment application cannot be used for any other purpose other than for the use it was provided for.

An employer is obliged to keep the documents accompanying the application at the applicant's disposal for a reasonable period of time (if the applicant has been rejected).

3.4.   PRE-EMPLOYMENT ENQUIRIES

By adopting the Act of 15 January 2018, Belgium introduced some form of regulation on pre-employment enquiries.

Indeed, the Belgian federal government has noticed that a discrimination complaint (based on protected criteria, such as age, race, gender or belief) rarely leads to criminal prosecution because it is very difficult for the Social Inspectorate to prove discrimination. Therefore, the Act of 15 January 2018 allows, as from 1 April 2018, the technique of mystery shopping/calling. It is made available to the social inspectors who are in charge of monitoring the respect of anti-discrimination laws to carry out tests in a company if:

– there are objective data that points to discrimination. According to the Act, a complaint or a report, supported by results of 'data mining and data matching', would suffice;
– the prior permission of a magistrate (labour auditor or Public Prosecutor) is required. This also allows the magistrate to indicate what strictly necessary (minor) criminal offences (e.g., the use of a false name) the social inspector may commit in the execution of his assignment.

Furthermore, mystery shopping/calling may only be used if there is no other way to prove discrimination. It is also explicitly forbidden for social inspectors to trigger or provoke certain behaviours or statements. After all, mystery shopping/calling should not result in creating a discriminatory situation and should be limited to creating the possibility of revealing a discriminatory practice.

For the moment, the procedure for mystery shopping and calling is rarely used in practice by the Social Inspection, as it is deemed too restrictive and too cumbersome to help to detect discrimination. However, a revision of the system is expected in 2022 in order to make the procedure more practical for the social inspectors. Under the new system, it is clear that data mining and data matching results are not a necessary (cumulative) pre-condition for mystery shopping and it clarifies that social inspectors can use this research method in any stage of an investigation as long as it is deemed proportionate in the context of the case.

An employer must also more generally respect privacy and anti-discrimination laws and cannot investigate a prospective employee's private life.

3.5.   PRE-EMPLOYMENT TESTS AND EXAMINATIONS

It is generally accepted that an employer can submit applicants to certain tests in order to obtain information about their abilities if these tests are job-relevant (e.g., tests with regard to the use of computers and various software, personality and IQ tests which the Belgian Data Protection Authority recommends to be carried out under the responsibility of a psychologist or, if the applicant agrees, by a person who has been properly trained by a psychologist to administer the tests). Practical tests may not take longer than the time required to test the applicant's competence.

All test-related costs must be borne by the employer.

The results of the tests must be kept confidential, and the processing of the obtained data requires the applicant's approval.

3.6.   BACKGROUND, REFERENCE AND CREDIT CHECKS

Extended background checks on employees are not common in Belgium. They should be limited to the strict necessity of assessing the applicant's professional skills relevant to the job offered. The most common background checks relate to education and past employment records and, in relation to employment with an international dimension, confirmation that the applicant has the appropriate permission to work in Belgium.

An employer is permitted to ask the applicant questions about his/her educational background that are genuinely relevant to the nature and working conditions of the job. In such a framework, an employer may therefore require the applicant to produce copies of academic certificates (*see* section 3.3).

An employer is also permitted to ask the applicant questions about his/her prior employment that is job-relevant. An employer can request an employment certificate – i.e., a document that needs to be delivered by a former employer, indicating the period of employment and the position of the employee concerned or the nature of the job performed – and, with the applicant's consent, contact his/her previous employer in order to ask questions about his/her job performance.

As a general rule, the employer may not ask questions about an applicant's credit and financial background. The general anti-discrimination Act of 10 May 2007 prohibits any discrimination based on personal wealth. Belgian law does not allow recruiters to have access to the financial information of applicants.

An employer can undertake social media/Internet checks if the general rules are complied with (i.e., no discrimination, in line with the GDPR, and genuinely relevant for the job). However, arguments of applicants invoking their 'right to privacy' when confronted with information extracted from the Internet will often be rebutted when they have put the information online themselves, and either had the intention to make certain information public or should have known that the posted information would become public.

Therefore, the use by an employer of information on LinkedIn should, in principle, not raise any issues as this social network is exclusively dedicated to business and professional relations, and one of its aims is to be identified by employers. The use of information posted on Facebook, on the other hand, can be more problematic as it may cover the private sphere, especially if the profile access is limited.

3.7. INTERVIEWING

Employers are only allowed to ask questions that are relevant to the job and do not violate privacy and anti-discrimination laws (*see* above sections 3.1, 3.2 and 3.6).

3.8. HIRING PROCEDURES

The hiring of an applicant is, in principle, not subject to any specific formality. It is, however, highly recommended to have a written employment contract stipulating at least the essential elements, such as the function and the remuneration. Further, certain work conditions or special provisions must be agreed in writing in order to be valid (e.g., a fixed-term contract, part-time work, and non-compete clauses: *see* section 2.2).

3.9. FINES AND PENALTIES

When the information gathered via background checks is used in a discriminatory way, compensation is due on a flat rate basis (six months' gross wages), or the employee can claim, from the potential employer, an indemnity for the actual damage suffered.

The GDPR foresees penalties rising up to EUR 20 million or 4% of a company's global turnover (Article 83). In addition, the Belgian Act of 30 July 2018 foresees penalties from EUR 250 up to EUR 15,000 for the data processor if he/she did not comply with its provisions.

3.10. CHECKLIST OF DOS AND DON'TS

- Only ask questions during the recruiting process that are strictly job-related.
- Avoid any direct or indirect discrimination based on legally protected grounds and respect the applicant's privacy.

- Treat the collected information as confidential and protect it from third-party access.
- Sign a written employment contract with all relevant stipulations.

4. MANAGING PERFORMANCE/CONDUCT

4.1. OVERVIEW

In an employment relationship, employees are subject to employers' managerial power, which means that it is the employer's responsibility and prerogative to organize the work and to issue orders.

In the performance of an employment contract, employees have a legal obligation to show respect and consideration for their employer. Furthermore, in accordance with the Employment Contracts Act, an employee must:

(1) carry out his/her work carefully, honestly and conscientiously at the agreed time and place and in accordance with the agreed conditions;

(2) act in accordance with the orders and instructions given to him/her by the employer in connection with the performance of the contract;

(3) refrain, both during the contract and after its termination, from:
  (a) revealing business secrets or manufacturing secrets or any personal or confidential information coming to his/her knowledge in the performance of his/her duties;
  (b) engaging or cooperating in any form of disloyal competition.

(4) abstain from anything that might prejudice his/her own safety or the safety of his/her colleagues, the employer or any other person;

(5) return, in good condition, any tools or unused raw materials that have been entrusted to him/her by the employer.

If the employee fails to respect these obligations, the employer may take disciplinary measures, but it is more common that this would be reflected in an evaluation document or in a written warning.

4.2. COACHING AND COUNSELLING

There is no general legal obligation on the employer to provide coaching and counselling to an employee when there is a problem with the performance or conduct of an employee. However, in some companies, and also in some sectors of industry, a prior warning must be given, or even an individual coaching plan must be proposed before dismissing an employee for reasons related to a lack of performance or the conduct of the employee.

There are, however, some legal provisions which encourage the continued vocational training of employees in general.

4.2.1   Training

Before the change in the legislation of 2017, the different sectors of industry needed to take the necessary initiatives to make sure that at least 1.9% of the employers' total wage bill was spent on continued vocational training of their employees.

Since 1 February 2017, a combined effort to ensure five days of training per year per full-time equivalent is envisaged for all Belgian companies together (i.e., an 'inter-professional goal'). Only companies of at least ten employees are subjected to a training obligation. The actual obligation in the execution of this inter-professional goal for each individual company depends on the existence of a CBA at the sectoral or company level.

Quasi all sectors have failed to negotiate CBA's regarding training targets. Therefore, the theoretic target of 1.9% was never transposed to the work floor. This absence of action resulted in new federal legislation in 2022, which grants an individual right of five training days (paid by the employer) to every employee.[12] Sectors can decrease this number with a minimum of two days. Companies with less than ten workers are exempted from this obligation and above ten but below twenty workers, the employee only has a right to one training day.

4.2.2.   Paid Educational Leave

This is a system that allows the employee to be absent from work for attending courses while continuing to be paid. As educational leave became a regional competence, the Flemish system has been applicable since September 2019. The other Regions are still following the federal system. The employee will receive his/her normal salary (capped at EUR 2,987 gross – figure for the school year of 1 September 2020 until 31 August 2021),[13] and the employer will be compensated for this by the competent administration.

Usually, it is the employee that takes the initiative for paid educational leave. The courses must not necessarily relate to the employee's function, but they have to be recognized by the competent Region.

---

12. 3 days as of 2022, 4 days as of 2023 and 5 days as from 2024.
13. The capped salary remains a federal competence.

4.3.   WRITTEN EVALUATIONS

It is common practice that companies establish a system for evaluating employee performances. This is often linked to a merit or bonus system.

As a result of the labour law reform of 2014, which imposed an obligation on employers to provide an explanation of their reasons for dismissal[14] (*see* section 5), written evaluations have become an important element in the proof of, e.g., performance issues.

Belgian law does not provide strict legal rules for written evaluations. However, employers need to consider the common rules regarding discrimination, privacy and abuse of rights. It is also recommended to offer employees the opportunity to defend their own views in case of a negative evaluation. If not, this might result in legal problems if the negative evaluation is followed by a dismissal.

4.4.   WARNINGS AND SUSPENSIONS

In Belgium, an employer may only inflict those sanctions upon an employee that are explicitly included in the Work Rules of the company (e.g., warnings, fines, suspension, etc.). It is not necessary to include a dismissal as a disciplinary sanction in the Work Rules as the Employer is granted a right to dismiss an employee by the Employment Contracts Act.

The Work Rules must contain: (i) the sanctions, amounts of fines and purposes to which they shall be attributed, together with the offences in respect of which they are imposed; and (ii) the possibilities of redress open to employees who have grievances, or who wish to make observations on, or object to, sanctions imposed on them.

The employer, or its representative, must communicate the sanctions to the employee on the first working day following the day on which the employer learned about the shortcoming. The name of the employee, date, reason and sanction must be registered.

A fine can never be higher than one-fifth of the employee's net salary and the money must be spent to the benefit of the employees (the actual destination must be laid down in the Work Rules).

Generally, suspensions are only accepted as a sanction in case the duration is limited to two or three days. According to case law, longer suspensions or demotions could give rise to a constructive dismissal, in which case the employer will be liable for an indemnity in lieu of notice (*see* section 5).

---

14. For all dismissals occurring after 1 Apr. 2014.

4.5.   CHECKLIST OF DOS AND DON'TS

– Make sure that the Work Rules of the company mention the disciplinary measures that may be inflicted upon the employees.
– Make sure that all evaluations and warnings are drawn up in the correct language (Dutch, French or German, depending on the location of the operational unit of the company). Non-compliance with the language legislation will render the documents null and void.
– Often, there are CBAs at the industry or company level, which determine specific procedures, which have to be complied with.
– If there is a Trade Union Delegation within the company, the latter will have the prerogative to be involved in a disciplinary procedure.

5.   TERMINATION OF EMPLOYEES FOR PERFORMANCE OR DISCIPLINARY REASONS

5.1.   OVERVIEW

Until 2014, an employer could terminate the employment contract of a white-collar employee without any obligation to justify its decision. For blue-collar employees, on the other hand, the employer had to prove reasons related to either the employee's competencies or conduct, or the operational requirements of the undertaking.

Since 1 April 2014, this difference in treatment with respect to the justification of the dismissal no longer exists, and the same rules now apply to blue- and white-collar employees. Under Belgian law, an employer may now only dismiss an employee for reasons which are connected to: (i) the employee's competencies (i.e., *the required skills for the job*) or his/her conduct/attitude (e.g., *inappropriate behaviour towards managers, colleagues or customers, repeated delays, failure to comply with the employer's instructions, etc.*); or (ii) the operational requirements of the undertaking (e.g., *rationalization of the organization, financial difficulties, lack of work as a result of the loss of a major account, etc.*).

Thus, it is permissible to dismiss an employee for lack of performance or disciplinary reasons.

The duration of the notice period or the indemnity in lieu of notice, however, depends only on the employee's seniority within the company. The fact that the dismissal is based upon performance or disciplinary reasons will not influence the duration of the notice period nor the amount of the indemnity in lieu of notice.

Only in the event of a serious cause may the employee be dismissed without any notice or indemnity in lieu of notice. A 'serious cause' is defined as a fault so serious that it renders the continuation of the working relationship immediately and definitely impossible (e.g., *theft, violence, fraud, etc.*). Employers need to bear in mind that the Belgian courts are rather reluctant to accept the application of dismissal for a serious cause, as this has severe consequences for the employee (no notice period, no severance pay, temporary exclusion of unemployment benefits).

In case of a termination for a serious cause, the employer needs to observe the following formalities:

– he must dismiss the employee within three working days of the day he became aware of the facts (serious misconduct); and
– he must inform the employee, by registered mail, of the grounds of his/her dismissal at the same time or within an additional period of three working days.

If these strict deadlines and formalities are not complied with, the dismissal for serious cause will be irregular, and an indemnity in lieu of notice will be due to the employee.

For any other dismissal, the general regime on the motivation of the dismissal applies. This regime consists of two principles:

(1) Each dismissed employee has the right to know the precise reasons which have led to his/her dismissal.

The obligation to inform an employee of the reasons which motivated a dismissal only exists when the employee has made a request to the employer to this extent.

The employee must address this request to the employer by registered mail within two months after the end of the employment contract or, in the case of a notice period to perform, within six months after the notification thereof, without exceeding two months following the end of the employment contract.

The employer's answer must explain the specific reasons on which the dismissal was founded.

(2) The dismissal of an employee hired in the frame of an open-ended employment contract must be carried through for reasons related to the employee's capability or conduct or to the operational requirements of the undertaking and must also have been decided upon by any other normal and reasonable employer if they were faced with the same facts. If these conditions are not met, the dismissal will be considered as 'manifestly unreasonable'.

The obligation to inform an employee of the reasons, which motivated the dismissal, applies to the dismissal of employees with at least six months of service. Furthermore, such an obligation is not applicable in the following situations:

(a) in the frame of an employment contract for temporary agency work (interim) or an employment contract for students;

(b) dismissal in view of retirement or of the regime of 'unemployment benefits with employer top-ups' (i.e., the former 'bridging pension');

(c) dismissal in the framework of a collective dismissal, closure or termination of the activity of the company or multiple dismissals as defined at an industry level;

(d) when a specific dismissal procedure must be complied with, prescribed by law or by CBA (e.g., employees' representatives); and

(e) dismissal for serious cause (the rules with respect to the obligation to motivate a dismissal do not apply, but the rules concerning the manifestly unreasonable dismissal are, however, fully applicable).

Finally, some employees enjoy special protection against dismissal. Generally speaking, there are two types of protected status:

(1) Employees that can only be dismissed for a limited number of reasons and for whom a specific preliminary procedure must be complied with.

There are three categories of employees that benefit from this form of protection:

   (i) the employees who were a candidate and/or elected to be an employee representative within the Works Council and/or the Health and Safety Committee (*See* section 9.5);

   (ii) the employees that are Trade Union Delegates (*See* section 9.5); and

   (iii) the Prevention Advisor, for whom the employer needs the permission of the Health and Safety Committee if there is no serious cause to dismiss.

(2) Employees that can be dismissed for any reason, as long as the reason is not linked to grounds for which they enjoy a protected status.

It concerns, e.g., employees on maternity leave, employees that filed an official complaint about moral or sexual harassment at work, employees that filed a complaint about discrimination at work, employees with reduced working hours in the framework of so-called time credit, employees who hold a public office, etc.

In general, for these employees, the employer needs to prove a sufficient reason for their dismissal, which is not linked to the reasons for which they enjoy a protected status. If the employer fails to prove such reasons, the employee will be entitled to a lump sum additional indemnity equal to, in principle, six months of salary.

5.2.   SEPARATION/SEVERANCE PAY

5.2.1.   Dismissal for Serious Cause

In the event of a serious cause, the employee may be dismissed without any notice nor indemnity in lieu of notice.

Employees that are dismissed for serious cause often try to challenge this decision in court. The judge will then have to evaluate whether or not the fault was serious enough to justify an immediate dismissal without notice or indemnity in lieu of notice. Furthermore, the judge will also verify whether all formalities were complied with.

If the judge decides that there were insufficient grounds for dismissal for serious cause, if the employer did not prove the reasons for the dismissal or if the formalities were not complied with, the dismissal for serious cause will be irregular, and an indemnity in lieu of notice will be due to the employee. However, there is neither a right nor an obligation to reinstate the employee.

5.2.2.   A Dismissal for Reasons Other than a Serious Cause

Employment contracts are generally terminated through the provision of a notice period or the payment of an indemnity in lieu of notice. A combination of both, where the serving of a notice period is followed by the payment of an indemnity for the remainder of the notice period, is also possible.

To be valid, notice must be given in writing and must specify the starting date and the duration of the notice period. If the employer terminates the contract, notice must be served by registered mail or by a bailiff. Moreover, notice must be given in the correct language.

Failing this, the notice may be deemed null and void. In that case, the employment contract will have been terminated without serving notice, so that the employer will be obliged to pay an indemnity in lieu of notice.

If the employment contract is terminated with the payment of an indemnity in lieu of notice, no specific formalities need to be complied with. The indemnity in lieu of notice is calculated on the basis of the annual salary of the employee at the time of termination, including statutory and contractual fringe benefits.

Before 1 January 2014, the notice periods for blue- and white-collar employees were very different.

Yet, the labour law reforms of 2013 resulted in equal notice periods (or indemnities in lieu of notice) for blue- and white-collar employees.

For the calculation of the legal notice period for dismissals that are notified on or after 1 January 2014, a distinction must be made between three different situations.

5.2.2.1. Open-Ended Employment Agreements Whose Performance Commenced on or After 1 January 2014

The notice periods are fixed by law and only depend on the employee's seniority. If applicable, any previous period during which the employee worked as a temporary agency worker for the same employer must be taken into account in the calculation of the seniority, with a limit of one year.

As a way to reintroduce a trial period, new notice periods are applicable since 1 May 2018 in case of dismissal by the employer during the first six months of employment. Nothing changes for the notice periods in case of resignation by the employee. In this case, the notice period will increase slower and is capped at thirteen weeks (when the employee reaches seniority of eight years or more).

The notice periods are expressed in weeks:

Start of the Notice Period During	Notice Period Employer	Notice Period Employee
< 3 months	1 week	1 week
<4 months	3 weeks	2 weeks
<5 months	4 weeks	2 weeks
<6 months	5 weeks	2 weeks
< 9 months	6 weeks	3 weeks
< 12 months	7 weeks	3 weeks
< 15 months	8 weeks	4 weeks
< 18 months	9 weeks	4 weeks
< 21 months	10 weeks	5 weeks
< 24 months	11 weeks	5 weeks
Years 2–3	12 weeks	6 weeks
Years 3–4	13 weeks	6 weeks
Years 4–5	15 weeks	7 weeks
Years 5-6	18 weeks	9 weeks
Years 6-7	21 weeks	10 weeks
Years 7-8	24 weeks	12 weeks
Years 8-9	27 weeks	13 weeks

Start of the Notice Period During	Notice Period Employer	Notice Period Employee
Years 9–20	+ 3 weeks per started year	13 weeks
Year 20	62 weeks	13 weeks
From year 21 on	+1 week per started year	13 weeks

Article 37/2 Employment Contracts Act.

If a more beneficial regime for the employee exists at the company or individual level, the more beneficial regime must be applied.

5.2.2.2. Open-Ended Employment Agreements Whose Performance Commenced Before 1 January 2014

The calculation of the notice period is conducted in two steps:

(1) the first step relates to the seniority within the company on 31 December 2013;
(2) the second step relates to the seniority as of 1 January 2014.

In summary, the result of the sum of the notice periods resulting from steps 1 and 2 equals the final notice period that must be observed.

For the *first step*, different rules apply depending on, among others, the status of the employee (blue/white-collar) and his/her level of remuneration:

– *White-collar employees earning EUR 32,254 gross or less on 31 December 2013.*
Save for some exceptions, the general rule is that the notice period for employers equals three months per started five-year period of service. For employees, the notice period is one and a half months in case of a seniority of less than five years. As of five years' seniority, it is three months.
– *White-collar employees earning between EUR 32,254 and EUR 64,508 gross on 31 December 2013.*
Save for some exceptions, the notice period for employers equals one month per started year of service, subject to a minimum of three months. For employees, the notice period is one and a half months per started period of five years seniority with a maximum of four and a half months (in case of ten years or more seniority)
– *White-collar employees earning more than EUR 64,508 gross on 31 December 2013.*

Save for some exceptions, the notice period for employers equals one month per started year of service, subject to a minimum of three months. For employees, the notice period is one and a half months per started period of five years seniority with a maximum of six months (in case of fifteen years or more seniority)

– *Blue-collar employees whose employment contract started before 1 January 2012.*

Save for some exceptions, the notice periods are as follows:

Seniority on 31 December 2013	Notice Period Employer	Notice Period Employee
<6 months	28 days	14 days
≥6 months and <5 years	35 days	14 days
≥5 years and <10 years	42 days	14 days
≥10 years and <15 years	56 days	14 days
≥15 years and <20 years	84 days	14 days
≥20 years	112 days	28 days

– Blue-collar employees whose employment contract started on or after 1 January 2012.

Save for some exceptions, the notice periods are as follows:

Seniority on 31 December 2013	Notice Period Employer	Notice Period Employee
< 6 months	28 days	14 days
≥ 6 months and < 5 years	40 days	14 days
≥ 5 years and < 10 years	48 days	14 days
≥ 10 years and < 15 years	64 days	14 days
≥ 15 years and < 20 years	97 days	14 days
≥ 20 years	129 days	28 days

For the *second step*, the above-mentioned notice periods for open-ended employment agreements whose performance commenced on or after 1 January 2014 apply.

5.2.2.3. *Employment Agreements for a Fixed Term or for a Specific Project*

For a termination during the first half of the agreed term of the employment contract (with a maximum of six months that has to be taken into account), the above-mentioned notice periods for open-ended employment contracts are applicable. The notice period has to end within the first half of the agreed term.

For consecutive fixed-term contracts, this rule can only be applied to the first contract.

For a termination in the second half of the agreed term, after six months or when the notice period for termination during the first half of the agreed term does not end in this first half, the employer is due to pay an indemnity in lieu of notice to the employee equal to the remuneration that should have been paid until the end of the agreed term. This amount may not exceed two times the amount of the indemnity in lieu of notice that is due in case of termination of an open-ended employment contract.

5.2.2.4. Compensatory Measures and Additional Support

As blue-collar employees whose employment contract started before 1 January 2014 will partially be subject to the consequences of the old regulations on notice periods, some compensatory measures were adopted to grant them additional social protection in case of a dismissal. These measures provide that upon meeting certain conditions, such employees will be entitled to a supplement payment by the National Unemployment Office. The blue-collar employees would be entitled to a so-called dismissal compensation payment covering the difference between the duration of their statutory notice period and the notice period they would have been entitled to if the new unified notice periods were to be applied for their seniority since the start of their employment contract.

Furthermore, the employer must offer outplacement support intended to encourage the redeployment of the employee. This obligation exists in general for all employees who are entitled to a notice period or indemnity in lieu of notice of at least thirty weeks. If the employment contract is terminated with a notice period, the employee must utilize this outplacement support during his/her working hours. In case the contract is terminated with an indemnity in lieu of notice, the employer may deduct four weeks' salary from the indemnity in lieu of notice.

If the dismissed employee is older than 45 years but is not entitled to a notice period of at least thirty weeks, the employer must also offer an outplacement package at its own expense.

5.2.3. Additional Indemnities in Case of Non-compliance with the Motivation Obligations

An employer that does not respond to an employee's request for the reasons for dismissal owes the employee a lump sum civil fine (indemnity) of two weeks' salary. This indemnity is exempt from social security contributions.

An employee dismissed in a manifestly unreasonable way may claim an indemnity of three to seventeen weeks' salary. The amount of indemnity depends on the unreasonableness of the dismissal. If the indemnity is granted through a court decision or provided in a settlement agreement, which is approved by a court decision, it will be exempt from social security contributions.

5.3. FINES AND PENALTIES

There are no criminal fines or penalties in case of violation of the legislation regarding the termination of employment contracts.

5.4. CHECKLIST OF DOS AND DON'TS

– Verify whether the employee benefits from a specific protected status (e.g., employee representative, Trade Union Delegate, Prevention Advisor, an employee on maternity leave, an employee who has filed a complaint about moral harassment, etc.).
– Verify whether a specific procedure exists at a company or an industry level that needs to be complied with before proceeding with the dismissal.
– Check the language legislation to make sure all communications are in the correct official language (Dutch, French or German, depending on the location of the operational unit of the company).
– Gather all necessary information to calculate the correct notice period, such as the seniority within the company and the salary.

6. LAY-OFFS, REDUCTIONS IN WORKFORCE AND/OR REDUNDANCIES AS A RESULT OF JOB ELIMINATIONS OR OTHER RESTRUCTURING

6.1. OVERVIEW

In this chapter, the focus will be on mass reductions in the workforce, as individual dismissals based upon economic reasons will follow the same regime as set out in section 5. This means that an economic reason is generally accepted as a ground for dismissal. In such cases, the notice period or the indemnity in lieu of notice is the same as specified in section 5.

Where multiple redundancies qualify as a collective dismissal, the legislation on collective dismissals applies, and possibly the legislation regarding the closure of undertakings.

A collective dismissal or a closure of undertaking triggers several specific obligations for the employer, such as:

– prior information and consultation obligations towards the employee representatives;
– several notifications towards the authorities;
– payment of specific indemnities; and
– redeployment initiatives.

6.2. REDUCTIONS IN WORKFORCE/LAY-OFFS/JOB ELIMINATIONS

6.2.1. Scope

A *collective* dismissal arises where a certain minimum number of employees are terminated during a continuous period of sixty days for reasons unrelated to the employee's performance or competence. The following table sets out the relevant number of employees:

Size of the Undertaking	Number of Dismissals
≥20 and <100	10 or more employees
≥100 and <300	10% (or more) of all employees
≥300	30 employees

An undertaking is defined as a so-called technical business unit (TBU). The assessment of what constitutes a TBU is based on economic and social criteria. As such, one TBU can comprise several legal entities, but it is also possible that within one legal entity, there are several TBUs. A division of the undertaking is, within the framework of this legislation, assimilated with a TBU.

In order to calculate the size of the undertaking, the total number of employees that have been declared to the social security authorities for each quarter of the previous calendar year must be divided by the number of quarters for which a social security declaration has been made.

There is a closure of undertaking if:

- there is a definite stoppage of the principal activity of the undertaking (or a division thereof); and
- the number of employees is reduced below one-fourth of the average number of employees who were employed in the undertaking during the four quarters preceding the definite stoppage of the activity.

Should a collective dismissal occur as a result of the closure of an undertaking, the employer will need to comply with the applicable procedures for both situations. Within the scope of this publication, we will focus on the employer's obligations in the event of collective dismissal.

6.2.2. Information and Consultation

6.2.2.1. Who Must Be Informed and Consulted?

The employer who intends to proceed with a collective dismissal has an obligation to inform and consult about such a decision with the employee representatives.

If there is a Works Council, the information and consultation take place with the Works Council. If there is no Works Council, the information and consultation take place with the Trade Union Delegation and if there is no Trade Union Delegation, with the Health and Safety Committee. If no such employee representative bodies exist within the company, the information and consultation must take place with the personnel or their 'ad hoc' representatives.

The information and consultation must take place prior to the decision on the planned change in structure.

6.2.2.2. The Content of the Information to be Disclosed

The consultation must relate to the possibilities to prevent or decrease the collective dismissal, as well as to the possibilities to alleviate the consequences by adopting social accompanying measures, in particular, those aimed at contributing to the relocation or retraining of the dismissed employees.

In this respect, the employee representatives must be provided with a written report announcing the intention to collectively dismiss, which also contains the following information:

- the reasons for the collective dismissal;
- the number of employees qualifying for dismissal and their categories;
- the number of employees usually on the payroll and their categories;

- the period during which the dismissals will be carried out;
- the criteria that will be taken into account for selecting the employees qualifying for dismissal; and
- the methods for calculating any extra-legal redundancy payments.

A copy of this report must be transmitted to the employee representatives, the Trade Union representatives, the Director of the subregional employment office and to the President of the executive committee of the Federal Employment Administration. This report must also be posted in the company.

6.2.2.3. At What Time Must the Employer Fulfil These Information and Consultation Obligations?

The information and consultation obligations must be fulfilled prior to the decision being taken. The employee representatives may therefore not be presented with a 'fait accompli', and the informing and consulting may not be reduced to a purely formal matter.

This information and consultation obligation must enable the employee representatives to expertly conduct discussions, during which they will be able to give advice and make suggestions and objections.

In practice, this means that the employer must first announce an intention to collectively dismiss and then hold several meetings with the employee representatives to consult about, among others, possibilities to avoid redundancies and measures that could at least mitigate the effect of the redundancies. The employer must allow the employee representatives to ask questions with regard to the intended collective dismissal and allow them to put forward arguments in that respect or to make counterproposals. Finally, the employer must examine and answer these questions, arguments and counterproposals.

The law does not stipulate how long this information and consultation period must take. The duration will depend on the willingness of the employee representatives to collaborate.

6.2.2.4. The Formal Notification of the Intention to Collectively Dismiss

As soon as the information and consultation obligations have been completed, and if the employer persists with its intention to collectively dismiss, it must notify the Director of the subregional employment office at the place where the employer is located and the President of the executive committee of the Federal Employment Administration, of the confirmation of its intention to collectively dismiss.

This notification must state:

- the name and address of the company;
- the nature of the activity of the company;
- the Joint Committee to which the company pertains;
- the number of employees on the payroll;
- the reasons for the dismissal;
- the number of employees who qualify for dismissal, including information about the employees' expertise, age bracket, professional category and department;
- the period during which the dismissals will take place; and
- the proof that the employer has satisfied the relevant legal conditions.

The employer must also send a copy of the notification of the intention to collectively dismiss to the employee representatives. Moreover, a copy is to be posted inside the company, and a copy is to be sent, by registered mail, to the employees affected by the collective dismissal and whose employment contracts have already terminated at the time of the posting.

It should be emphasized that if the collective dismissals were to be accompanied by the closure of the company or a division thereof, additional formalities must be complied with. Additional conditions may also be imposed at the industry level.

6.2.3.   The Social Plan

6.2.3.1. In General

The employer may not dismiss the employees concerned by the collective dismissal until after the expiry of a term of thirty days, commencing on the date of the confirmation of the intention to collectively dismiss. The Director of the subregional employment office may extend the term of thirty days to a maximum of sixty days.

This period is often used to negotiate a social plan. Even though there is no legal obligation to do so, employers and Trade Union organizations generally work out a social plan, granting the affected employees additional compensation and other measures aimed at reducing the impact of the collective dismissal. The following items are often part of a social plan:

- Extra-legal end-of-contract indemnities, often in proportion to the employee's seniority within the company.
- A scheme for older employees (55+) providing an additional allowance paid by the employer on top of the unemployment benefits until their retirement (the system of unemployment benefits with employer top-ups, formerly called 'bridging pension').

- Reconversion premiums for employees accepting a different job within the company.
- Job security for the employees not involved in the dismissals.

6.2.3.2. The Legal Indemnities to Which the Employees Are Entitled

In general, the dismissed employees are entitled to a notice period or indemnity in lieu of notice, calculated in accordance with the rules set out in section 5.

Furthermore, in some cases, the dismissed employees will also be entitled to an additional special indemnity for collective dismissals. For the purpose of the payment of this special indemnity, a collective dismissal is defined as a mass lay-off, taking place during a period of sixty days and affecting the following number of employees:

Size of the Undertaking	*Number of Dismissals*
0–20	Not applicable
20–59	6
60–...	10%

This indemnity is to be paid by the employer on a monthly basis for a maximum period of four months after the expiry of the notice period or the period covered by the indemnity in lieu of notice. The period during which the employee will be entitled to this additional indemnity depends on the duration of the notice period or the period covered by the indemnity in lieu of notice. If the employee was granted a notice period or receives an indemnity in lieu of notice amounting to seven months of salary or more, this special indemnity will not be due.

The special collective dismissal indemnity amounts to half of the difference between the last net monthly salary (capped), on the one hand, and, on the other hand, the unemployment benefits received. This special indemnity is not due to employees who are entitled to the special closure indemnity.

Furthermore, employee representatives enjoy special protection against dismissal. Their employment contracts can only be terminated on specific grounds and following a specific procedure.

These procedures need to be complied with, not only in case of an individual dismissal but also in case of collective dismissal, if the employer wants to avoid paying the 'protection indemnities' (*see* section 9.5).

6.2.3.3. *Outplacement Guidance Within the Context of a So-Called Redeployment Cell*

In the case of collective dismissals concerning employers who employ more than twenty employees, a redeployment cell aimed at the activation of the dismissed employees must be instituted. The redeployment cell must make an outplacement offer to the employees who are dismissed and who participate in the redeployment cell. Also, temporary agency workers or employees with a fixed-term contract may participate if their contract is not renewed as a result of the restructuring.

An employer employing twenty employees or less is only obliged to institute a redeployment cell if it wishes to dismiss employees within the framework of early retirement (system of unemployment benefits with employer top-ups) at an age lower than the age that is normally applicable for early retirement within the company.

Dismissed employees must participate in the redeployment cell for a period of three months for employees younger than 45 and six months for employees at least 45 years old. During this period, the indemnity in lieu of notice is paid to the employee in monthly instalments under the form of a so-called redeployment indemnity. The termination of an employment contract with a notice period is only possible in the following circumstances:

– the period covered by the redeployment indemnity is shorter than the notice period; and
– the employment contract is terminated after the period that exceeds the duration of the period covered by the redeployment indemnity.

6.3. FINES AND PENALTIES

If the information and consultation obligations are not correctly executed by an employer, the employer could, among others, be liable for a criminal fine of EUR 400–EUR 4,000, multiplied by the number of employees that are made redundant, with a maximum of EUR 400,000.

6.4. CHECKLIST OF DOS AND DON'TS

(1) Preparation is key in these matters. Therefore, take the time to:
   (a) define a communication strategy;
   (b) draft a budget for the social plan; and
   (c) prepare for a contingency plan.
(2) Comply with the language legislation.

(3) Verify all information shared with the employee representatives. Incorrect information could result in a lack of confidence and thus hinder the negotiations.

(4) Involve the external delegates from the Trade Unions present within the company from the start of the process.

(5) Attempt to make the employee representatives sign a statement that you have correctly carried out the information and consultation obligations before starting the negotiations of the social plan.

7. LABOUR AND EMPLOYMENT LAW RAMIFICATIONS UPON ACQUISITION OR SALE OF A BUSINESS

7.1. OVERVIEW

There was no specific legal framework on this subject in Belgium before the EU adopted Council Directive 77/187/EEC (now Directive 2001/23/EC), with a view to safeguarding employees' rights in the event of transfers of undertakings, businesses or parts of undertakings or businesses.

The Directive has been transposed into Belgian law by CBA No. 32*bis* of 7 June 1985, which has been amended several times.

CBA No. 32*bis* maintains employees' rights in the event of 'any change of employer arising from a conventional transfer of undertaking or part of an undertaking'. Employees' rights are therefore safeguarded in the event of a sale and/or acquisition of a business. The rules that apply to both types of transactions are the same and will be summarized under the heading 'Acquisition of a Business'.

7.2. ACQUISITION OF A BUSINESS

Three elements are essential for a transfer of undertaking to fall within the scope of CBA No. 32*bis*:

(1) The transfer must entail a change of employer.

(2) The transfer must relate to an undertaking or a division of an undertaking, i.e., an economic entity defined as 'any grouping of persons and assets enabling the exercise of an economic activity pursuing a specific objective and which is sufficiently structured and independent', provided that this economic entity maintains its identity and pursues its economic activity as a 'going concern' after the transfer.

(3) The change of employer must occur as a result of a legal transfer or merger. The type of agreement affecting the change does not matter so

that any sale and/or acquisition of a business will be covered, whatever contractual form it takes. On the other hand, transactions that do not imply a change of employer, such as share purchase agreements, are outside the scope of CBA No. 32*bis*.

Before the formal decision to transfer may be adopted, the transferring employer (the transferor) and the new employer (the transferee) must inform their respective employee representative bodies, i.e., the Works Council, or in the absence thereof, the Trade Union Delegation, or in the absence thereof the Health and Safety Committee (the so-called Committee for Prevention and Protection at Work) about the proposed transfer. The employees must be informed individually about the proposed transfer in case: (i) there is only a Health and Safety Committee; or (ii) there are no employee representative bodies within the undertaking.

The information must include the following elements:

– The agreed or proposed date for the transfer.
– The reason(s) for the transfer.
– The legal, economic and social consequences of the transfer for the employees concerned.
– The measures envisaged vis-à-vis the employees.

The transferor and the transferee must also consult the employee representative bodies, in particular with regard to the repercussions on the employment prospects for the personnel, the work organization and the employment policy in general. Consultations are not binding upon the employer.

There is no specific timeframe for the information and consultation process, provided that it takes place before the formal decision on the planned transfer is taken.

Failure to comply with this obligation would render the employer liable to criminal sanctions (a fine of EUR 400–EUR 4,000, multiplied by the number of employees employed in the company, up to a maximum of EUR 400,000), in accordance with Article 196 of the Penal Social Code.

In the event of a transfer within the framework of CBA No. 32*bis*, the rights and obligations of the transferor that originate in the employment contracts existing on the date of transfer are automatically transferred to the transferee. The automatic transfer takes place despite any contrary intention or contractual agreements between the transferor and the transferee.

As a consequence:

– the employee whose employment contract has been terminated by the transferor with the granting of a notice period and who is still performing this notice period at the moment of the transfer of (the division of) the undertaking within which he/she is employed will be transferred to the transferee;

– the transferor and the transferee cannot validly determine that only part of the employees concerned will be taken over by the transferee.

As from the transfer date, the transferee must respect all essential employment conditions (including remuneration, job status, acquired seniority, place of work and working conditions) of the transferred contracts. The transferee is not permitted to modify any such condition unilaterally after the transfer date. If the transferee fails to comply with this provision, the transferred employees could claim damages or invoke that their employment contract was terminated by the transferee (constructive dismissal) and claim an indemnity in lieu of notice.

However, there is one exception with regard to extra-legal pension schemes to which CBA No. 32*bis* does not apply. As a consequence, there will be no automatic transfer of these schemes, and it will be up to the transferor and the transferee to negotiate extra-legal pension arrangements for the transferred employees, with the understanding that the employees must be granted an 'equivalent benefit' if the pension scheme is not continued after the transfer.

In principle, and unless the transfer would entail serious modifications to an essential element of their employment contract, the employees may not oppose the transfer.

A refusal on the part of the employees could be considered as an implicit resignation. Alternatively, the transferee could also dismiss the employees concerned for a serious cause.

The transferee who wishes to harmonize the essential employment conditions with those of its own employees may do so through the conclusion of addenda to individual employment contracts or by entering into a CBA at the company level, which must respect the imperative rules of law or CBAs at the national and industry level.

A transfer of undertaking also triggers the continued application of CBAs applicable to the transferor. However, when the transferor and the transferee pertain to different Joint Committees, it is generally admitted that the transferee will not continue to be bound by the CBAs, which have been entered into within the Joint Committee of the transferor. The transferee must, however, respect the employment conditions included in such CBAs at the time of the transfer, as they are incorporated within the employment contracts that have been transferred.

After the effective transfer date, the transferee becomes solely liable for all debts resulting from the transferred employment contracts, including payment of indemnities in the event of dismissal of any of the transferred employees. For debts existing at the date of transfer (e.g., salary arrears), the transferor and the transferee will both be liable vis-à-vis the transferred employees and the National Social Security Office.

The transferor and the transferee may not dismiss the affected employees solely because of the transfer. This prohibition concerns the dismissal related to the transfer and any dismissal occurring a short time before or after the transfer, provided that it is related to the transfer. However, dismissals may still take place for a serious cause or for economic, technical or organizational reasons entailing changes in the workforce. The right to dismiss for reasons other than the transfer of business remains unaffected.

Any employee illegally dismissed by the transferor will have the possibility to introduce a court proceeding against both the transferor and the transferee in order to obtain the payment of a termination indemnity and/or damages (the illegality of the dismissal does not render the dismissal null and void). Case law generally sets the amount of damages at about EUR 5,000.

The effect of the transfer on the employees' representatives depends on several criteria (e.g., whether the transferred undertaking maintains its autonomy as a distinct operational unit). In any event, Belgian law guarantees the continuity of the representation functions and protects the transferred employees' representatives against dismissal.

7.3.   ACQUISITION CHECKLIST

Before proceeding with an acquisition, it is important that the transferor and the transferee inform and consult the representatives of their respective employees that will be affected by the acquisition.

Although the transfer is automatic, it is nevertheless advisable to:

– notify each employee concerned by the transfer in advance and in writing;
– confirm the employee-related modalities of the transfer in an Employee Transfer Agreement. These modalities may relate to the effective date of the transfer, the employees concerned by the transfer, their remuneration and working conditions, the applicable CBAs and the transferor's and transferee's liabilities before and after the transfer date.

If it is unclear whether CBA No. 32*bis* applies, it is strongly recommended to conclude a tripartite transfer agreement between the transferor, the transferee and each of the individual employees. This is particularly recommended for undertakings in the service sector, which rely heavily on manpower.

Once the transfer has occurred, it is better to avoid different terms and conditions applying to the transferred employees and the initial employees of the transferee. Therefore, it is recommended to harmonize the terms and conditions of all (transferred and existing) employees through a company CBA or individual addenda to the existing employment contracts.

7.4.   SALE OF A BUSINESS

See section 7.2 above; these are the same consequences as acquisitions.

7.5.   SALE CHECKLIST

See section 7.3 above; these are the same consequences as acquisitions.

8.   USE OF ALTERNATIVE WORKFORCES: INDEPENDENT CONTRACTORS, CONTRACT EMPLOYEES AND TEMPORARY OR LEASED WORKERS

8.1.   OVERVIEW

In Belgium, alternative workforces may take various forms and are increasingly used so as to reduce costs while providing companies with working relationships that are more flexible than those based on traditional employment contracts.

Employers that do not wish to enter into a traditional employment contract may call upon independent contractors and, more generally, have recourse to subcontracting. They may also employ temporary (agency) workers or leased workers from other employers subject to very strict conditions, which will be detailed hereinafter.

8.2.   INDEPENDENT CONTRACTORS

8.2.1.   Definition

Independent contractors are referred to as 'self-employed workers' in Belgium. A self-employed worker is any individual performing professional activities within the scope of which he/she does not work under the authority of an employer.

Consequently, the criterion for distinguishing between a self-employed person and an employee is based on the existence or the absence of a link of subordination between the contracting parties: if one of these parties exercises the employer's authority over the other, the employment relationship is deemed to be an employment contract.

A situation in which parties qualify their employment relationship as a self-employed relationship, while in practice, one party exercises the employer's authority over the other, is referred to as false self-employment and is used by employers to avoid the application of the stringent (protective) rules of labour law, and to avoid the payment of substantial social security contributions and the withholding of income tax on wages.

8.2.2. Creating the Relationship

The Employment Relations Act of 27 December 2006 (the '2006 Act') created a legal framework to ascertain the legal nature of the employment relationship.

The basic thought of this 2006 Act was that parties could freely choose the nature of their employment relationship. However, the factual performance of the contract must be in line with its content. If factual elements are found to be incompatible with the qualification chosen by the parties, the contract can be requalified (from self-employed to employee).

The 2006 Act defines four general criteria to be used in determining whether such factual elements exist in a particular case:

(1) *The parties' intention as expressed in the agreement.* The qualification decided upon by the parties will be the starting point for the judge's analysis regarding the nature of the contract. However, it is understood that the actual performance of the agreement must be in line with the nature of the employment relationship chosen by the parties.

(2) *The worker's freedom to organize his/her own working time.* The following elements point towards a link of subordination: the obligation to strictly comply with work schedules, the reporting of any absence, etc.

(3) *The worker's freedom to organize his/her work.* In the framework of self-employment, parties enjoy a wider degree of freedom regarding the organization and the practical execution of the work (complete freedom to choose the dates of annual leave, freedom to determine how the work will be performed, etc.). However, it is accepted that general guidelines may be given to accommodate the requirements of the job itself (e.g., the opening and closing hours of a shop, which, although placing an obligation on an independent contractor, does not necessarily indicate subordination).

(4) *The ability to exercise hierarchical control.*

In addition to these general criteria, the 2006 Act also provides for neutral criteria that are not relevant for determining the nature of the employment relationship. Such neutral criteria are, among others, the title of the contract, registration with a social security office, registration with the 'Crossroads Bank for Enterprises' (*Kruispuntbank der Ondernemingen – Banque-Carrefour des Entreprises*), registration with the value-added tax (VAT) administration and the way in which revenue is reported to the tax authorities.

Also, the use of an intermediary company structure (e.g., a management company of the independent contractor) does not in itself exclude the existence of an employment relationship if the principal were to exercise the employer's authority over the person behind the company.

Finally, the 2006 Act entitles the government to list specific socioeconomic criteria for a determined sector or profession or categories of professions. These specific criteria apply in addition to the criteria listed above and may not deviate from them.

Such specific criteria have been determined for six sectors of industry, namely the construction sector, security sector, transportation sector, cleaning sector, agricultural sector and horticultural sector. For these sectors, a rebuttable presumption exists that an employment contract is entered into if at least five out of the list of nine specific criteria are fulfilled.

In 2022 a new specific rebuttable legislative presumption was introduced for the digital platform economy.

If it appears that, in practice, a link of subordination exists between the 'principal' and the person rendering the services, the self-employed agreement may be requalified by a court as an employment contract.

In such a case:

– the employer may be held fully liable for the entire amount of social security contributions that should have been paid (i.e., 13.07% employee's contributions and 27% employer's contributions[15] on the fees paid) to be increased with interest, penalties and an increase of 10%. There is no possibility for the employer to recover the amounts paid from the employee concerned. These arrears can be claimed for the last three years (seven years in case fraud is proven);
– in addition, the employer could be held liable for not having made personal income tax deductions. Tax increases and fines can be imposed. However, if deductions have not been made, and unlike in the case of social security contributions, the employer will not become solely liable for the taxes. If the authorities claim the payment of the taxes from the employer, the latter will have recourse against the employee for the amounts paid (provided that the employee is still solvent);

---

15. *See* s. 10.5.2.

– in case the employee claims the requalification of the agreement, arrears on salary (end-of-year premium) and holiday pay are due for the last five years;
– moreover, a criminal fine or an administrative fine can be imposed.

8.2.3. Compensation

The independent contractor will receive a fixed or variable fee. Fixed fees (as well as the reimbursement of expenses) may point towards a relationship of employment but are not decisive factors as long as the general criteria are met.

The independent contractor is responsible for paying his/her own social security contributions and taxes.

8.2.4. Other Terms and Conditions

The independent contractor must be registered with the Belgian company register called the 'Crossroads Bank for Enterprises' (*Kruispuntbank der Ondernemingen – Banque-Carrefour des Entreprises*). In many cases, he/she must also have a VAT number. Finally, he/she must also be registered with a social insurance fund.

Companies benefit from a higher degree of flexibility when working with independent contractors. As a rule, an independent contractor does not benefit from any legal protection granted by Belgian employment laws (especially with regard to termination). If the self-employed contract does not include any specific provisions with regard to termination, case law will be taken into consideration to determine the termination rights based on ordinary (as opposed to employment) contract law (notice period, compensation).

On 1 December 2020, the 'B2B' Act of 4 April 2019 entered into force.[16] This act has the purpose of offering a certain level of protection to a professional yet economically weaker party against the economically stronger party when concluding a contract. This protection is also applicable when a company hires an independent contractor. In short, the Act offers three types of protection mechanisms, which are considered to be of public order. First, there is a 'catch-all' provision that prohibits every clause in a contract which creates a manifest imbalance between the rights and

---

16. The Act of 4 Apr. 2019 regarding the revision of the Code of Economic Law concerning the abuse of economic dependency, illegitimate clauses and unfair market practices between companies, *MB* 24 May 2019.

obligations of the parties. Second, there is a 'black list' of four clauses that are always prohibited:

(1) Purely discretionary conditions: irrevocable commitment of one party while the performance of its obligations is subject to a condition the fulfilment of which depends exclusively on the will of the other party.
(2) Unilateral interpretation: the unilateral right to interpret one or another clause of the contract.
(3) Waiver of legal recourse: in the event of a dispute, to have the other party waive any recourse against the company.
(4) Fictitious knowledge: to irrefutably establish the knowledge or acceptance by the other party of clauses of which he/she was not able to take cognizance before the conclusion of the agreement.

Third, there is a 'grey list' of eight clauses that are presumed to be illegitimate; however, this presumption can be refuted:

(1) Unilateral Variation Clauses: granting the undertaking right to alter unilaterally the price, characteristics or terms of the contract without a valid reason.
(2) Tacit fixed-term renewal clauses: tacitly extending or renewing a fixed-term contract without giving a reasonable period of notice to prevent the renewal.
(3) Shift of economic risk: transferring, without consideration, the economic risk to one party when it would normally be borne by the other party to the contract.
(4) Undue limitation of recourse: to improperly exclude or limit the legal rights of a party in the event of a breach of contract in whole or in part breach or defective performance by the other party of any of its contractual undertaking of any of its contractual obligations.
(5) No reasonable notice: to bind the parties without specifying a reasonable period of notice.
(6) Undue limitation of liability: to exonerate the company from its liability for its wilful misconduct, its gross negligence or that of its agents or, except in cases of force majeure, for failure to perform the essential obligations which are the subject of the contract.
(7) Limitation of means of evidence: limiting the means of evidence that the other party may rely on.
(8) Disproportionate damages: in the event of non-performance or delay in performance of the obligations, to fix amounts of compensation that are clearly disproportionate to the harm that might be suffered.

8.3. CONTRACT WORKERS

Belgian legislation allows subcontracting provided that the initial contract from which specific tasks are subcontracted does not explicitly indicate that it is to be performed exclusively by the main contractor.

The main contractor, as well as his/her subcontractors, are each responsible for their own employees to whom they give instructions and whose wages and social security contributions they pay. The authority of the main contractor and his/her subcontractors towards their respective employees cannot be shared or leased except in the specific cases where it is allowed by law (*see* below).

Belgian law imposes specific obligations on the principal, the main contractor and his/her subcontractors:

– The Act of 12 April 1965 provides for a mechanism of joint liability for the payment of salary where the main contractor or his/her subcontractors seriously fail to fulfil their responsibilities concerning the payment of remuneration in due time to their employees. This mechanism is only valid for specific sectors such as the construction, cleaning and food sectors.
– The Act of 12 April 1965 provides for a mechanism of joint liability for the payment of salary to employees of non-EU countries residing illegally in Belgium. This mechanism is valid for all sectors.
– The Act of 27 June 1969 provides for a mechanism of joint liability for the payment of social security contributions for the main contractor or the subcontractors that are indebted towards the National Social Security Office. This mechanism is only valid for the building, private security and meat sectors.

The same mechanism of joint liability exists for these sectors with respect to the reimbursement of debts towards the income tax service.

8.4. LEASED WORKERS

8.4.1. Principle of Prohibition

Under Belgian law, the leasing out of employees is governed by the Act of 24 July 1987 on temporary work and the hiring-out of workers.

In principle, Article 31 of this Act prohibits a natural or legal person from leasing his/her employees to third parties who use those employees and exercise any part whatsoever of the employer's authority over them. The violation of this prohibition can lead to civil, criminal and administrative sanctions.

8.4.1.1. Civil Sanctions

- The employment contract between the employee concerned and the employer (i.e., the entity which leases the employee) is void as of the moment the employee starts working for the 'user'.
- The user and this employee are bound, as of that moment, by an open-ended employment contract.
- The employee can terminate this contract without notice nor indemnity until the date on which he/she would normally no longer be at the disposal of the 'user'.
- The user and the employer (i.e., the entity which leases the employee) are jointly liable for the payment of social security contributions, remuneration and benefits deriving from this open-ended employment contract.
- Moreover, according to case law, the user may refuse to settle the bill of the employer based on the agreement whereby his workers would have been unlawfully leased out as such an agreement can be considered null and void.

8.4.1.2. Criminal or Administrative Sanctions

Generally, a criminal fine ranging from EUR 800 to EUR 8,000 can be imposed for each and every employee concerned by the leasing. However, the total amount of the fine cannot exceed EUR 800,000. Alternatively, an administrative fine, the amount of which ranges from EUR 400 to EUR 4,000 per leased employee with a maximum of EUR 400,000, can be imposed.

8.4.2. Exceptions

The Act of 24 July 1987, however, provides for some exceptions. In certain cases, exceptional leasing of employees is permitted, provided that a number of general conditions comply with (*see* section 8.4.2.1) and are conditional upon the warning to (section 8.4.2.2) or the prior authorization (section 8.4.2.3) of the Labour Inspectorate.

8.4.2.1. General Conditions (To Be Fulfilled Simultaneously)

- *Exceptional character.* The leasing of employees must have an exceptional character, which means that it must be limited in time and may not be repetitive, i.e., not be exercised in a regular manner. It is thus possible to consider that leasing of employees is exceptional when it is unique and justified by circumstances, which excludes that the leasing of employees could be regarded as an activity in itself.

– *Permanent employees.* The leased employees must be permanent employees, i.e., persons who are already employed by the employer who leases them and who regularly work for the employer.
– *Level of remuneration.* The remuneration and fringe benefits of the leased employees cannot be inferior to the remuneration and fringe benefits of the employees carrying out the same functions within the user company.

8.4.2.2. Leasing of Employees Conditional upon Prior Information to the Labour Inspectorate

If the above-mentioned general conditions are fulfilled, the leasing out of employees is permitted in two hypotheses, provided that the Social Inspectorate is informed of this leasing beforehand:

(1) Within the framework of a collaboration between companies of the same economic or financial entity (groups, holdings).
(2) For the execution, on a temporary basis, of specialized tasks requiring a specific professional qualification.

In both hypotheses, the signing of a written document by all parties prior to the leasing of employees is required.

8.4.2.3. Leasing of Employees Conditional upon Prior Authorization of the Labour Inspectorate

If the above-mentioned general conditions (section 8.4.2.1) are fulfilled, it is possible to obtain authorization for the leasing of employees from the Labour Inspectorate. To this end, the following procedure must be complied with:

– The user must first obtain the agreement of the Trade Union Delegation within its company or, failing that, of the employees' organizations represented in the competent Joint Committee.
– In possession of this approval, the user can then introduce an authorization request to the Labour Inspectorate.
– The conditions and duration of the leasing of an employee must be recorded by a written document signed by the employer, the user and the employee before the start of the leasing of the employee.

8.4.2.4. Consequences of a Leasing of Employees Permitted by Law

The leasing of employees not only implies that the contract between the employee and its employer continues to be valid and in force, but also that the user becomes jointly liable with the employer for the payment of social security contributions, remuneration, indemnities and benefits, which derive from the employment contract.

8.4.3.   Alternatives

An alternative to working with leased employees is to rely upon temporary work or temporary agency work in accordance with the conditions set out in Chapters 1 and 2 of the Act of 24 July 1987.

Temporary work is the activity performed within the framework of an employment contract, with the aim of replacing a permanent employee, responding to temporary work overload or performing work of an exceptional nature.

In the frame of temporary agency work, an employment contract is entered into between a temporary work agency (interim office) and an employee. The employee then carries out temporary work of the kind described above for a client of the agency (the user). Temporary agency work may also be reverted to for integration purposes, in the sense that it is allowed to lease interim employees to users with the aim of providing these employees a permanent job with the user at the end of the leasing period.

Since 1 February 2017, temporary work agencies can, in principle, also conclude an open-ended employment contract with an interim employee, which is then supplemented with separate 'customer contracts' between the temporary work agency and the user.

Another alternative to the leasing of employees is to set up a so-called employer's association (*werkgeversgroepering* – *groupement d'employeurs*). In the frame of such an 'employer's association', two or more companies can jointly hire (an) employee(s) who will work for the different members of the association. The association may not employ more than fifty employees. The employee enters into one single employment contract with the association, which leases the employee to its different members. The different members will be jointly liable for all payments to the employee (wages, etc.) and third parties (the social security office, tax authorities, etc.). The employer's association must comply with certain legal formalities and must be approved beforehand by the Minister of Work. Recent reforms in 2013 and 2017 have liberalized the very strict conditions, which used to apply to the types of organizations allowed to perform that activity, as well as to the profiles of the employees who may be hired.

A final alternative to the leasing of employees is to have recourse to a service agreement between the companies concerned. Within such a framework, a user company may only give limited instructions to employees of a service provider working within the user company pursuant to a service agreement executed between the user company and the employer/service provider. The subject of the said agreement is not to lease out employees but, rather, the execution of predetermined work.

However, the following conditions must be met simultaneously:

– The service agreement must be in writing and must clearly list the exact types of instructions that the user company can give to the service provider's employees (the types of instructions will depend on the work to be performed and on the functions concerned; e.g., attendance at meetings, preparation of documents on a determined topic, respect for deadlines, etc.).
– These instructions may not undermine the legal employer's authority over the employees.
  However, instructions given by the user regarding its legal obligations with regard to well-being at work (health and safety) are allowed.
– The factual situation must correspond with the language of the service agreement.

If any of these conditions are not met, there will be a prohibited lease of personnel.

8.5. CHECKLIST OF DOS AND DON'TS

– When two parties enter into a self-employed working relationship, it is crucial that a well-drafted service agreement is entered into, clearly indicating the parties' intention to work together on a self-employed basis and highlighting the fact that the self-employed worker is free to organize his/her work and working time. However, a well-drafted contract is not enough to avoid a requalification of the contract into an employment contract. The factual performance of the contract must be in line with its formal content. In some sectors of industry, the principal should also be careful in its selection of main contractors and subcontractors, as the law provides for mechanisms of joint liability for the payment of salary, social and fiscal contributions.
– In case of a service contract between two companies, in the frame of which employees of the service provider work on the premises of the undertaking of the user to execute the work agreed upon, it is very important that the agreement explicitly and in detail lists the types of instructions that may be given by the user to the employees of the service provider. If not, there may be a question of prohibited leasing out of personnel.

9. OBLIGATION TO BARGAIN COLLECTIVELY WITH TRADE UNIONS: EMPLOYEES' RIGHT TO STRIKE AND A COMPANY'S RIGHT TO CONTINUE BUSINESS OPERATIONS

9.1. OVERVIEW OF UNIONS' RIGHT TO ORGANIZE

9.1.1. Freedom of Association

The right of freedom of association is established in Article 27 of the Belgian Constitution, as well as Article 3 of CBA No. 5. The Act of 24 May 1921, which also relates to the freedom of association, stipulates that no one can be forced to join an association. Any employer pressuring an employee to join or not to join a Trade Union will be liable for criminal sanctions. Closed shops and non-union shops are outlawed in Belgium.

Furthermore, the right to freedom of association is acknowledged in various international treaties to which Belgium is a party, such as the Universal Declaration of Human Rights (Article 23.4), the International Labour Organisation Conventions No. 87 and 98, the International Covenant on Economic, Social and Cultural Rights (Article 8.1), the European Convention for the Protection of Human Rights and Fundamental Freedoms (Article 11.1), the Revised European Social Charter (Article 5) and the Charter of Fundamental Rights of the EU (Article 12.1).

In Belgium, there are no restrictions regarding the creation of a Trade Union. However, only a few Unions, considered as a representative, are granted a specific role and specific rights by law. The three main representative Unions are as follows:

(1) The Belgian General Federation of Labour (*ABVV – FGTB*).
(2) The Confederation of Christian Unions (*ACV – CSC*).
(3) The Central Organisation of Liberal Trade Unions of Belgium (*ACLVB – CGSLB*).

In certain fields, the Belgian National Confederation of Executives and Managerial Staff (*NCK – CNC*) is also considered a representative Union.

As their names suggest, the above-mentioned Unions federate several smaller Trade Union organizations, traditionally competent in a given geographical area and within a set branch of activities (sector).

The rate of Union membership in Belgium is relatively high in comparison with other European countries (49% in 2019).[17] Behind the five Scandinavian countries, this is the next highest rate among Organisation for Economic Co-operation and Development countries.

---

17. Latest data for Belgium of 2019 by OECD/AIAS ICTWSS database, last update on 9 June 2021, www.oecd.org/employment/ictwss-database.htm

The most important rights of representative Trade Unions include the power to:

- enter into CBAs with one or more employers or representative employers' organizations;
- put forward candidates for elections to the Works Council and the Health and Safety Committee (the so-called Committee for Prevention and Protection at Work);
- ensure that the correct procedure is observed for the election of employee representatives;
- depending on the circumstances, form a Trade Union Delegation within the company;
- propose lay judges to sit on the Labour Tribunals and Labour Courts of Appeal.

Trade Unions in Belgium have no formal legal status or corporate capacity. As a result, Trade Unions only exist as legal entities to perform specific acts that are assigned to them by law. They can, e.g., represent their members before Labour Courts or, in some circumstances, engage in legal action on their own behalf in order to defend the interests of their members. Trade Unions, but not their members, essentially enjoy immunity from responsibility, which means that they cannot be held liable for (economic) damages as a consequence of a strike.

Employers are also organized. The most important employers' organization in Belgium is the Federation of Enterprises in Belgium (*VBO – FEB*). It is organized on a national scale, and its members are the various employers' organizations that are each active in a specific industry. In addition, several regional employers' organizations exist.

9.1.2.   The Right to Strike

Although widely accepted, the right to strike is not included in the Belgian Constitution, nor has it been formally adopted in Belgian legislation, despite numerous attempts to do so. In this respect, a 'gentlemen's agreement' was concluded on 18 February 2002, between the representative employers' organizations and the Trade Unions, in an attempt to informally agree on the limits of the right to strike in Belgium. The application of this gentlemen's agreement in practice has proven to be unsuccessful.

The right to strike is, however, acknowledged in several international instruments to which Belgium is a Member State (e.g., Article 6.4 of the revised European Social Charter). In addition, the right to strike was confirmed by the Supreme Court in 1981.

Consequently, the right to strike in Belgium is shaped via jurisprudence.

It is defined in a negative way, in the sense that certain acts that accompany strikes are prohibited, delimiting the fundamental right to strike.

The way in which a strike is executed will often determine whether the strike is proportional and therefore justifiable. A judge will not make a judgement regarding the opportunity of the strike (whether the reasons for going on strike are valid or not) but will only consider whether the execution of the strike is not disproportionate and does not excessively violate the rights of others. A judge will undertake such an assessment by balancing the following interests and subjective rights of the various parties:

– The right of the striking employees to strike.
– The freedom of the employer to conduct its business.
– The property right of the employer.
– The non-striking employees' right to work.
– Any rights of third parties.

In this framework, 'acts of violence' (*feitelijkheden – voies de fait*) committed during a strike (e.g., picketing accompanied by acts of violence against individuals or property, the occupation of business premises or the blocking of access roads) may be prohibited and subject to a financial penalty.

To this end, the employer can refer the matter to the President of the Court of First Instance (civil court, and not the Labour Tribunal) in order to obtain an injunction against such acts of violence. This procedure will be conducted as an interim injunction (*kortgeding – demande en référé*) or as an interim injunction by means of ex parte proceedings (*eenzijdig verzoekschrift – requête unilatérale*). In the latter procedure, no adversary party will be summoned for a hearing (often because no adversary party can be identified), and the absolute necessity of the procedure will have to be proven.

The right to strike is, in principle, not subject to any form of authorization or procedural requirements. However, in certain sectors of industry, CBAs include particular procedures that must be observed (e.g., an obligation to notify the employer beforehand). That being said, even in the absence of any such procedure, the failure to give prior notification of a strike to the employer could result in a sanction on the basis of the abuse of a right.

A striker has no right to a wage, but an employee affiliated with a Union will receive a 'strike indemnity' if the Trade Union agrees to the strike.

In principle, the participation in a strike may not be invoked as a serious cause, justifying the termination of the employment contract without a notice period or an indemnity in lieu of notice. However, when a striker acts violently during a strike, a dismissal for a serious cause can be justified.

Minimum service is guaranteed for certain activities in the public and private sectors, i.e., the education sector or the public health sector. The specific modalities that apply to the minimum service in these sectors of industry are fixed in the concerned Joint Committees. If these rules at the industry level are violated, penal sanctions can be applied.

The Act of 29 November 2017 introduced the continuity of the service within the public railway transportation sector in case of strikes. The Act foresees a duration of eight days between the announcement of the strike by the Unions and the date of the strike. The service is guaranteed by volunteers, i.e., persons not willing to take part in the strike, who must notify their intention beforehand. This gives the possibility to the public railway company to set up an adapted transportation plan which must be communicated to the public at least twenty-four hours in advance. Since then, a similar system has been introduced for prison guards (2019) and for the Flemish public transport company De Lijn in 2021.

In Belgian labour relations, lockout is rarely used.

9.2. RIGHT OF EMPLOYEES TO JOIN UNIONS

9.2.1. Collective Bargaining

Belgium has a long-standing tradition of social dialogue and the 'Social Partners'; i.e., the employers' organizations and the Trade Unions are involved in the majority of decisions in labour-related issues. Most employers' organizations and representative Trade Unions have a seat in the National Labour Council (where collective bargaining at the national level takes place) and the Joint Committees (committees at the industry level where CBAs are negotiated).

Additionally, CBAs can also be agreed upon at a company level, between the employer and one or more Trade Unions.

9.2.2. Representative Bodies at a Company Level

At a company level, several types of employee representation exist. The representative bodies that must be set up within Belgian undertakings if certain conditions are met are the Works Council, the Health and Safety Committee (the so-called Committee for Prevention and Protection at Work) and the Trade Union Delegation.

Works Councils must be set up in undertakings employing, on average, at least 100 employees (*see* below section 9.4). It is designed to foster information, consultation and collaboration between the employer and employees on technical, economic, financial and social issues. For instance, the employer is obliged to provide the Works Council with economic and financial information concerning the undertaking at regular intervals. The Works Council also has a right to be informed (and in some cases consulted) of the employment structure of the undertaking, any planned changes and their consequences to the workforce, as well as of employment matters such as work organization, collective dismissals or closure, etc.

A Health and Safety Committee must be set up in undertakings normally employing, on average, at least fifty employees. This Committee plays an advisory role in health and safety matters and is also closely involved in the recruitment of Prevention Advisors.

A Trade Union Delegation must be established at the request of one or more representative Trade Unions in undertakings employing the relevant minimum number of employees as determined by a CBA. The employer has an obligation to accept this request. The competencies of the Trade Union Delegation include matters relating to industrial relations (supervision of the observing of employment legislation), the presenting and discussing of individual and collective grievances and negotiations for concluding CBAs. In the event that there is no Works Council, a number of tasks of the Works Council are transferred to the Health and Safety Committee and/or the Trade Union Delegation.

The notion of 'undertaking' is to be understood as a 'TBU', i.e., an entity having a certain social and economic autonomy, whereby the social criteria are considered more important than the economic criteria. A TBU does not necessarily correspond to a legal entity (incorporated company).

According to an EU Directive and its implementation in Belgium, employees of large multinational companies based in Belgium with a presence elsewhere in the European Economic Area (EEA) have a right to ask for a European Works Council (EWC) to be set up. An EWC is a body that represents employees of a multinational company within the EEA in discussions with management on transnational issues.

9.3.   How Employees Select Unions

Both the Works Council and the Health and Safety Committee are composed of an employer's delegation and an employees' delegation. The employer's delegation consists of one or more acting or substitute members designated by management and chaired by the head of the undertaking.

The employee representatives within the Works Council and the Health and Safety Committee are Union members, nominated by their Union and elected within the frame of social elections, which must be organized by the employer every four years.

The members of the Trade Union Delegation are employees of the undertaking who are either appointed by the Unions or elected by the other unionized employees of the undertaking (although not in the frame of social elections).

9.4.   PRE-ELECTION CAMPAIGNING

The obligation to set up a Works Council exists as soon as the TBU 'usually and on average' employs at least a hundred employees. The obligation to set up a Health and Safety Committee applies when the usual average employment headcount comprises at least fifty employees.

This average workforce is calculated over a reference period that corresponds to the period from 1 October 2018 to 30 September 2019 for the social elections of 2020. In principle, one full-time employee who has been working in the undertaking during the complete reference year equals one employee for the calculation of the threshold. There is, however, a special calculation method for part-time employees and temporary agency workers.

The election process is strictly prescribed by law and starts 150 days prior to the actual election day. At several moments during the preparation process of the elections, the employer is required to communicate certain information and decisions against which employees can lodge an appeal.

A key moment during the electoral process is the 120th day before the election day. This is the start date of the so-called hidden protection period. During this hidden protection period, candidates for the social elections already benefit from retroactive protection against dismissal, while the employer is not yet informed of their candidacy.

9.5.   PROTECTION AGAINST DISMISSAL

Elected employee representatives and candidates for the social elections enjoy special protection against dismissal. Their employment contracts can only be terminated on specific grounds and following a specific procedure:

(1) Employees who were a candidate or hold a mandate within the Works Council or the Health & Safety Committee can only be dismissed for:
  (a) a serious cause (*see* section 5), which must be authorized in advance of the dismissal by the Labour Court; or
  (b) for technical and/or economic reasons that need to be approved in advance by the competent Joint Committee.
(2) In case the protected employee is dismissed without prior approval of the competent body, substantial damages will have to be paid by the employer. The amount of damages varies depending on whether or not the employee demands to be reinstated in his/her former position.

55

(3) If no reinstatement is requested, the damages will be equal to:
  (a) the gross remuneration for two years if the employee has less than ten years of service with the same employer;
  (b) the gross remuneration for three years if the employee has between ten and less than twenty years of service with the same employer;
  (c) the gross remuneration for four years if the employee has at least twenty years of service.

(4) If reinstatement is requested by the employee but refused by the employer, the damages that need to be awarded will be even higher. In addition to the two, three or four years of remuneration, the employee will also be entitled to damages equal to the employee's full remuneration up to the date on which a new Works Council or Health and Safety Committee is installed.

(5) Also, members of the Trade Union Delegation may not be dismissed for reasons related to the exercise of their mandate. In case of dismissal of a Trade Union Delegate on grounds justifying the dismissal (e.g., economic reasons or restructuring of the company), a specific procedure needs to be complied with. In most sectors of industry, damages amounting to one-year remuneration are due in case the procedures are not correctly abided by.

9.6. RELOCATION OF WORK/SHUTDOWN OF BUSINESS

In case of a transfer of an undertaking (or a division thereof) or collective dismissal, prior information and consultation obligations apply towards the employee representatives. Failure to comply with these obligations would render the employer liable for criminal sanctions (a fine of EUR 400–EUR 4,000, multiplied by the number of employees employed in the company, up to a maximum of EUR 400,000). For a more detailed overview, *see* section 7.2 (transfer of undertaking) and section 6.2 (collective dismissal).

9.7. CHECKLIST OF DOS AND DON'TS

– Invest in social dialogue with the Works Council, the Health and Safety Committee, the Trade Union Delegation and the Unions to avoid collective labour disputes or to have them settled promptly.
– The employer must provide the necessary means to the employee representatives in order for them to be able to execute their mandate in a proper way (e.g., an adequate room to organize the monthly meetings of

the Works Council and the Health and Safety Committee, a notice board for their publications, a number of paid hours off for Union activities, etc.)
- Be extra prudent and diligently comply with the stringent procedure applicable for the dismissal of an employee representative in the Works Council or the Health and Safety Committee, a non-elected candidate or a Trade Union Delegate. If not, you risk paying very elevated indemnities.
- Verify whether or not the threshold is reached for your company to be obliged to organize social elections and make sure that all steps within the electoral process are taken in a timely manner.

10. WORKING CONDITIONS: HOURS OF WORK AND PAYMENT OF WAGES – BY STATUTE OR COLLECTIVE AGREEMENTS

10.1. OVERVIEW OF WAGE AND HOURS LAWS

10.1.1. Wages

In principle, minimum wages are fixed per sector of industry in CBAs. Yet, these minimum wages may not be lower than the guaranteed average minimum monthly pay, fixed by a national CBA (*see* section 10.2). However, this does not prevent higher salaries from being paid to employees on the basis of the company or individual agreements or in response to the labour market. For managerial functions that are often excluded from the scope of the CBAs at the industry level setting the minimum wages, it is common practice that their salary packages are the result of negotiations between employer and employee.

In addition to their monthly gross salary, employees are entitled to a single (i.e., normal salary) and double holiday pay. Moreover, in most sectors of industry, the payment of an end-of-year premium (frequently equal to a salary of one month) is mandatory.

Employees are often granted fringe benefits on top of their salaries, such as meal vouchers, eco-vouchers, a company car or a mobility budget, an extra-legal pension plan (group insurance), hospitalization insurance, a bonus, and (stock) options (*see* section 12).

Only part of the salary, in principle one-fifth of the total gross income, may be paid in kind (e.g., housing accommodation, payment of utilities such as gas, water, and heating). Since 1 October 2016, salary can no longer be paid in cash, and employers are obliged to pay the employee via a bank transfer.

Article 157 of the Treaty on the Functioning of the European Union imposes the principle of equal pay between male and female employees for equal work. Translated into Belgian law, CBA No. 25, rendered obligatory by Royal Decree, imposes equal pay for men and women for equal or equivalent work. The text of this CBA No. 25 is to be added to the Work Rules of the company. The Belgian legislature took additional measures in order to fight against the wage gap between men and women. These measures include the industry level (the CBAs and function classification systems at the industry level must be gender-neutral, which is checked by the Employment Ministry) as well as the company level. Companies that employ at least fifty employees are required to undertake a biannual analysis of their remuneration policy in order to determine whether it is gender-neutral or not.

To enhance the competitiveness of the Belgian economy, the 'Social Partners', i.e., the Unions and employers' organizations at the national level, need to enter into so-called inter-professional agreements (IPAs), which set the maximum margin for wage cost development for the coming two years. The IPA is then later formalized in a national CBA rendered obligatory by Royal Decree. If no agreement can be reached, the government itself determines the maximum margin by Royal Decree. In 2019, the maximum margin for wage cost development in 2019 and 2020 was set by Royal Decree (as the Social Partners could not reach an agreement) at 1.1%. The maximum margin for 2021 and 2022 was set at 0.4% by the government after failed IPA negotiations.

Failure to comply with the maximum margin for wage cost would render the employer liable for administrative fines (a fine of EUR 250–EUR 5,000, multiplied by the number of employees employed in the company, up to a maximum of EUR 500,000). The employer needs to take the maximum margin for wage cost development into account 'on average', i.e., for all the employees of the company together.

10.1.2.   Working Time

In principle, the maximum working time is thirty-eight hours per week. Yet, this maximum may be lower in some sectors of the industry on the basis of a CBA.

The weekly working time schedule that can be applied in undertakings is either thirty-eight effective hours per week (or the lower limit set at the industry level) or thirty-eight hours on average over a specified reference period (e.g., the performance of forty hours per week with the allocation of twelve compensatory rest days over a one-year reference period in order to attain thirty-eight hours on average).

Under certain conditions, flexible working time schedules with a weekly working time exceeding thirty-eight hours may be introduced, provided that the quarterly or yearly average remains at thirty-eight hours per week.

The daily statutory maximum is eight hours per day. This can be increased to nine hours if additional weekly rest periods are foreseen (besides Sunday) or to ten hours in cases where the travel time between work and home is significant.

There are several statutory exceptions to this rule. In case of shift work, for instance, it is possible to work up to eleven hours per day (and fifty hours a week) and in case of continuous work, even up to twelve hours per day (and fifty hours per week), provided that a quarterly or yearly average of thirty-eight hours per week (or the lower limit set at the industry level) is respected.

The daily minimum working time is three hours, but statutory exceptions exist.

Apart from a few legal exceptions, such as urgent work necessary because of unforeseen circumstances, work may not be performed outside the working time schedules included in the Work Rules.

In principle, overtime is prohibited, although there are several exceptions to this rule (*see* hereunder section 10.3).

Working at night (between twenty and six hours), on Sundays, and during Public Holidays is in principle prohibited and is only allowed in a few strictly regulated cases.

10.2.   MINIMUM WAGE

In principle, minimum wages are fixed per sector of industry in CBAs. Yet, these minimum wages may not be lower than the guaranteed average minimum monthly pay, fixed by national CBA, which amounts to EUR 1,806.16 (figure as from 1 April 2022). Before 1 April 2022, there was a lower average minimum monthly pay for employees younger than 20 years old, but the distinctions based on age were abrogated, except in respect of the separate minimum wage for minors and students.

In many sectors of industry, the sectorial minimum wage is a lot higher than the guaranteed average minimum monthly pay that must be respected when, at the industry level, no CBAs are entered into.

10.3. OVERTIME

In principle, overtime is prohibited. Yet, there are several exceptions to this rule, in which case overtime is permitted, such as, among others, in the event of:

– an extraordinary increase in workload;
– work to deal with the threat of an accident or with an accident that has occurred;
– urgent work on machinery or equipment;
– urgent work necessary because of unforeseen circumstances;
– taking stock and preparing the accounts.

In certain circumstances, for overtime, the employer needs:

– the prior agreement from the Trade Union Delegation within the company and from the Labour Inspectorate (e.g., in case of an extraordinary increase of workload);
– the prior agreement from the Trade Union Delegation or, if this is not possible, to inform this body afterwards and to notify the Labour Inspectorate afterwards within a certain timeframe (e.g., in case of urgent work necessary because of unforeseen circumstances);
– voluntary overtime, at the request of the concerned employee, without the necessity to provide a specific reason and capped to a maximum of 100 hours per year (360 hours per year in case of a sectoral CBA rendered obligatory by Royal Decree).[18] During the pandemic, an additional 120 hours of voluntary overtime was granted in 2021 and 2022.

In most cases where overtime is authorized, compensatory rest periods must be granted to ensure that the normal weekly working time (thirty-eight hours or a lower limit determined by CBA) is complied with over a reference period. In principle, this reference period is three months but can be extended to one year by Royal Decree, a CBA, or in the Work Rules. In case of voluntary overtime, there is only a right on overtime pay but not on compensatory rest. Voluntary overtime must respect a weekly limit of fifty hours and eleven hours per day.

In principle, for work performed in excess of the limits of nine hours per day and forty hours per week (or lower limits determined by a CBA involving an effective reduction of daily or weekly working time), the employees will also be entitled to overtime pay as a supplement to their normal salary. If, however, weekly working time is thirty-eight effective hours (and the employees thus perform thirty-eight hours of effective work

---

18. During the COVID-19 pandemic, this limit was temporarily increased for certain essential sectors.

per week), hours worked in excess of the thirty-eight hours give the employees the right to overtime pay.

Overtime pay is at least 1.5 times the employee's regular rate of pay and twice his/her regular rate if the overtime is performed on a Sunday or a Public Holiday.

In some circumstances, additional compensatory rest may replace overtime pay. This must be provided by a CBA. Every hour entitling a person to an extra pay of 50% must be replaced by at least half an hour of rest and any overtime with a bonus of 100% by at least one hour.

10.4. MEAL AND REST PERIODS

In between two working days, the employee is entitled to eleven consecutive hours of rest. This rest period of eleven hours comes on top of Sunday rest so that the employee is entitled to a total rest period of thirty-five consecutive hours.

As of the performance of six consecutive hours of work, the employee is entitled to a break.

The duration and modalities of the break are determined by CBAs. In the absence of a CBA, a break of a minimum of one-quarter of an hour must be granted to the employees.

10.5. DEDUCTIONS FROM WAGES

10.5.1. Permitted Withholdings on Salary

Withholdings on employees' salaries are limited by the Act of 12 April 1965 on the protection of workers' wages and salaries to the following payments or contributions:

– tax withholdings, employee's social security contributions, and any contributions for the financing of complementary social security benefits, which can be deducted by virtue of individual agreements or CBAs;
– fines imposed by the Work Rules;
– indemnities due by the employee if he/she is liable for causing damage as a result of fraud, a serious fault, or a frequently appearing minor fault (Article 18 of the Employment Contracts Act);
– advance payments by the employer;
– the amount of the warrantee, the employer may ask for to secure the obligations of the employee; and

– the surplus payment in case an employee performed too few hours in reference to the average weekly working time in the flexible working time system (*glijdende uurroosters – heures flottants*) at the end of a given reference period or upon the termination of the employment contract.

The total amount that can be withheld on the employee's salary may – in principle – not exceed one-fifth of the employee's salary after deduction of the advance tax payments, social security contributions, and additional social security benefits. This limitation to one-fifth of the employee's salary does not apply in cases of fraud or resignation by the employee.

10.5.2.   Social Security Contributions

Unless stated otherwise by an international agreement, employees working in Belgium for an employer established in Belgium, or an operational office in Belgium, will in principle, be subject to the Belgian social security scheme for employees.

In this scheme, both employees and employers have to pay contributions to the National Social Security Office (*RSZ – ONSS*). The employer's contributions always amounted to approximately 32.40% for white-collar employees and around 38.40% for blue-collar employees. Yet, in mid-2015, the Belgian federal government reached an agreement on 'guidelines' of a tax shift from labour to other forms of income. The 'Tax shift Act' of 26 December 2015 outlines the first steps of this agreement. One of the key reforms has been the drop in employer's social security contribution to 30% since 1 April 2016 and to 27% since 1 January 2018 (still the case in 2022).

Yet, numerous measures to promote employment have resulted in a reduction of the amount of the social security contributions of certain target groups, such as older employees, long-term jobseekers, and first hires.

The employee's contributions are fixed at 13.07% and are deducted from his/her gross salary. The resulting amount corresponds to the taxable salary from which the withholding tax is deducted. The withholding tax constitutes an advance tax payment. Depending on the level of the annual salary and the employee's family situation, there are two kinds of scales applicable to married persons/cohabitants or single persons. The annual tax rates applicable to employee income range from 25% to 50%.

10.6.   GARNISHMENT

The monthly net amount of the employee's salary can be subject to garnishment and transfer, but only to a limited extent (figures for 2022):

- Under EUR 1,186.00: nothing.
- Between EUR 1,186.01 and EUR 1,274.00: 20%.
- Between EUR 1,274.01 and EUR 1,406.00: 30%.
- Between EUR 1,406.01 and EUR 1,538.00: 40%.
- As of EUR 1,538.01: 100%.

These income limits are increased by EUR 73 (figure in 2022) for each dependent child.

The limits do not apply when the transfer or garnishment is done on account of non-observance of maintenance obligations (alimony).

10.7. Exemptions to Wage and Hour Laws

Rules relating to working hours and overtime do not apply to, among others:

- employees in a managerial role or a position of trust within the company. The functions that can be regarded as managerial functions or positions of trust are enumerated within the Royal Decree of 10 February 1965. Some examples are: company executives, assistant executives, managers, engineers, shop supervisors, and warehouse managers. The list within the Royal Decree is obsolete and therefore gives rise to discussions:
- sales representatives;
- domestic servants;
- homeworkers (incl. teleworkers).

This implicates that for the above employees, the daily and weekly working time limits and the rules with regard to rest periods and breaks do not need to be respected. These employees may perform night work and will not receive overtime pay or compensatory rest for overtime hours they may perform.

Yet, the rules with regard to Sunday rest will apply to the first three categories of employees (employees in a managerial role or a position of trust, sales representatives, and domestic servants). Homeworkers, however, may perform work on Sundays and Public Holidays.

It is highly recommended to expressly stipulate in the employment contract of the above categories of employees that the agreed salary is deemed to cover all hours worked, including any overtime hours. Indeed, according to a trend in case law, employees within the above-mentioned positions can be entitled to their normal salary for overtime work (i.e., 100% instead of 150% and without compensatory rest) in the event that the employment contract does not expressly exclude such payment.

10.8. CHILD LABOUR

The statutory minimum age for the employment of children is 15 (except if they are still subjected to full-time compulsory education, in which case the minimum age can be 16). Individual exceptions are possible in view of performances as an actor, singer, dancer, model, etc. These exceptions are strictly regulated.

Specific rules also apply for young workers (minors between 15 and 18):

- they may not perform work that surpasses their abilities, threatens their health, or endangers their morality;
- they benefit from more protective rules with regard to working time limits, rest periods, and breaks (e.g., breaks of 30 minutes as of the performance of 4.5 hours a day and breaks of 1 hour in cases of 6 hours' work and rest periods of 12 hours between two working days);
- they may only perform overtime hours, night work, and work on Sundays and Public Holidays in a limited number of exceptional circumstances and subject to certain conditions.

Royal Decrees can extend all of these rules to young employees between 18 and 21 years of age.

10.9. RECORDKEEPING REQUIREMENTS

10.9.1. Information That Must Be Maintained

(1) Prior to the commencement of the activities, the employer must ask every employee to produce an identity document, verify this document for its authenticity and validity, and retain a copy of it in the employee's file.

(2) In order to be able to fill in the personnel register or the DIMONA application[19] and to include all obligatory specifications on the individual payslips and on the overview of the yearly earnings (*see* section 10.9.2), the employer must collect and maintain, among others, the following human resources and payroll information with regard to its employees: the name, address, identification, and social security number of the employee, the date of entering into service, the days and hours worked, the days of suspension of the employment

---

19. DIMONA stands for 'Immediate declaration of employment' and is meant to provide the social security office with information about the commencement and termination of employment agreements for social security purposes.

contract of the employee and the reasons for this suspension (illness, holiday, paid leave, etc.), and the basic salary and fringe benefits.

(3) Upon termination of an employee, the employer must issue the following documents to the employee: an employment certificate (indicating the date of termination), a C4-form (this is an unemployment certificate including all relevant information with regard to the past employment and the reason for termination), and a vacation certificate for white-collar employees (to verify whether all amounts have been paid and allowing the employee to determine his/her right to annual holidays from his/her new employer).

(4) Although not obligatory, it is advisable for an employer to keep personnel records that include:
   (a) evaluation forms;
   (b) written warnings;
   (c) performance sheets, etc.

This information will be useful when determining upon a bonus payment or a promotion, to build up a file for dismissal (for a serious cause or other), etc.

10.9.2.   Records That Must Be Retained

The most important mandatory documents that each employer in Belgium should possess with regard to the personal file of its employees are as follows:

– A *registry* of all the employed *personnel* in the company (*personeelsregister* – *registre de personnel*). This is, however, not necessary for employers who declare their personnel electronically via the DIMONA application. A special personnel registry (on paper or electronically) is required when the employees are employed at different locations.

– *Individual payslips* (*loonfiche* – *fiche de paie*): on paper or electronically. If an employee works in a flexible hour system, the employer is required to provide the employee with an overview of his/her current amount of worked hours in comparison with the daily and weekly hour schedule in the company at the same time.

– Individual *overview of the yearly earnings* of each employee (*individuele rekening* – *compte annuel*).

– Specific *employment contracts*, such as employment contracts for students, temporary work, or fixed-term work.

– The daily *work schedules* of part-time employees with variable hours, as well as the sheets, which make mention of the performed hours outside the planned schedule (*afwijkingsblad – document de contrôle*).
– All documents related to the employment of *foreign employees* (work permit, LIMOSA notification).

These documents need to be kept at the workplace for a period of at least five years (with the exception of the sheets which make mention of the performed hours outside the planned schedule for part-time employees, which only need to be kept for one year, and the documents related to the employment of foreign employees, which need to be kept for the complete duration of the employment).

Moreover, a Belgian employer is also obliged to keep a number of mandatory documents pertaining to health and safety rules, such as, among others:

– *A Global Prevention Plan.* In this five-year plan, the results of the company's risk analysis and the prevention activities to be developed and adopted with regard to safety and health need to be programmed, taking into account the size of the company and the nature of the risks attached to the activities of the company.
– *Yearly Action Plan.* This plan works out the Global Prevention Plan on a yearly basis.
– *Yearly report* on the activities of the *Internal Service* for Prevention and Protection at Work (ISPPW).[20]
– *Written agreement with the External Service* for Prevention and Protection at Work[21] concerning the tasks, which are bestowed on the External Service (*identificatiedocument – document d'identification*).
– An internal *emergency plan* with information on escape routes, security drills, instructions in case of an emergency, etc.
– A standard *form for industrial accidents* (*arbeidsongevallensteekkaart – déclaration d'accident*) as well as each completed version of this form relating to a specific industrial accident. The filled-in forms must be kept in the company for at least three years after the employment contract with the concerned employee was terminated.

10.9.3.   Failure to Maintain Required Records

– Criminal or administrative fines can be imposed for infringements of these recordkeeping requirements. The amount of each fine depends on the level of severity, which the law ascribes to a specific infringement. It

---

20. *See* s. 13.
21. *Ibid.*

ranges between EUR 400 and EUR 48,000, to be multiplied by the number of concerned employees, but with a maximum of the hundredfold of the imposed sanction. For some infringements, six months to three years of imprisonment is, in principle, also possible.

– Criminal prosecution is, however, rather exceptional. In the event that the Labour Prosecutor decides not to prosecute, the official report of the Labour Inspectorate will then be sent to the Administrative Fines Office within the Ministry of Employment. This office will then have to decide whether or not to impose an administrative fine.

– However, usually (but this can vary from case to case), the competent authorities first request to take remediating action and only if no sufficient action is taken is a criminal or an administrative fine imposed.

10.10.   REDUCTIONS IN COMPENSATION CAUSED BY ECONOMIC DOWNTURN

The compensation of employees can only be reduced with their consent. Any unilateral reduction of the salary, even in case of an economic downturn, would be illegal, and the employee concerned could claim payment of arrears. It may also give rise to a constructive dismissal, implicating that the employee can consider the employment contract as being terminated by the employer, entitling him/her to an indemnity in lieu of notice.

Yet, Belgian labour law provides the possibility for employers facing a shortage of work due to the economic situation to reduce the working time or suspend the contract of their employees for a certain period of time. This is the so-called system of temporary lay-offs, which mainly applies to blue-collar employees. It can also apply to white-collar employees, but only if the company is recognized as an undertaking facing financial difficulties (e.g., in case of a substantial drop of a minimum of 10% of the turnover, the production or the orders during a reference period) and provided that certain conditions are met (a CBA at the industry or company level or an approved company plan must be in place).

During the temporary lay-off periods, employees are not entitled to their salary but to unemployment benefits paid by the National Unemployment Service (*RVA – ONEM*). In addition, all employers (or the Social Fund at the industry level) will have to pay their white-collar employees in a temporary lay-off, a minimum additional benefit determined in the CBA or the company plan (and with an absolute minimum of EUR 2.00 per day).

The introduction of a temporary lay-off period in the company requires various previous formalities, such as notifying the employees' (representatives) and the Unemployment Services.

During the COVID-19 pandemic crisis of 2020–2022, the system of temporary unemployment was simplified, so all companies that were forced to close down or that experienced a drop in work could put their workers (blue-collar and white-collar) on temporary unemployment due to force majeure (COVID-19). The Belgian employers have used this system en masse during the crisis. The employees receive a higher benefit than usual from the National Unemployment Service. This temporary system is supposed to stop in the second half of 2022 (but has been continuously prolonged).

10.11. CHECKLIST OF DOS AND DON'TS

– Verify if wages and working time hours are in line with minimum standards included in the CBAs at the industry level.
– Companies employing at least fifty employees are obliged to make a biannual analysis of their remuneration policy in order to determine whether it is gender-neutral or not.
– Any contemplated salary increase may not exceed the maximum margin for wage cost development set by the Belgian government.
– All working time schedules need to be included within the Work Rules.
– Make sure that overtime hours are only performed in the cases permitted by law and that – apart from some exceptions – both compensatory rest and overtime pay are granted.
– Insert a clause within the employment contracts of employees in a managerial role or a position of trust, sales representatives, and homeworkers stipulating that the agreed salary is deemed to cover all hours worked, including any overtime hours.

11. OTHER WORKING CONDITIONS AND BENEFITS: BY STATUTE, COLLECTIVE AGREEMENTS OR COMPANY POLICY

11.1. HEALTH AND OTHER INSURANCE

Employees are not entitled to any insurance, besides the insurance provided by the mandatory Belgian social security system for employees, which covers:

– old-age and survivor's pensions;
– unemployment benefits;
– insurance for accidents at work;
– insurance for occupational diseases;

- family allowances;
- healthcare, sickness and disability benefits;
- annual vacation (only for blue-collar employees; white-collar employees are paid by their employer).

Additional benefits may be included within CBAs at the industry or company level or within individual employment contracts.

Employers often grant their (managerial) employees a supplementary pension plan (*see* hereunder section 11.2) and/or hospitalization insurance on top of the social security benefits.

11.2. PENSION AND RETIREMENT BENEFITS

The statutory retirement age in Belgium is officially 65 years; however, this age will increase to 66 by 2025 and to 67 by 2030 (Act of 10 August 2015).

The retirement age is the same for men and women. This was different in the past, but over the years, the retirement age for women has been gradually raised to the same level as that of men.

Retired employees receive a pension from the Belgian social security system.

The amount of the retirement pension depends on the employee's period of employment in Belgium, as well as on his/her salary during that time, adjusted for the cost of living at the time of calculation of the pension. For each year the employee has worked, one forty-fifth of the full pension rate will be taken into account.

The retirement pension amounts to a maximum of 60% of the employee's average pay over his/her career (ceiled). However, this amount can be increased to 75% if the employee has a dependent spouse.

The yearly guaranteed minimum old-age pension (*gewaarborgd minimumpensioen – pension minimum garantie*) for employees with dependents amounts monthly to EUR 1,804.88 and EUR 1,444.36 for single employees (figures for 2022).

Retired employees are permitted to work subject to an earnings ceiling.

If employees meet certain conditions regarding age and length of career, they can benefit from an early retirement pension. In 2021, employees with employment of forty-four years can retire at 60, employees with employment of forty-three years can retire at 61 and employees with employment of forty-two years can retire at 63. Exceptions exist for labour-intensive professions and in the case of long careers.

Under the system of unemployment benefits with employer top-ups (the former 'bridging pension'), the employee will receive unemployment benefits from the social security system and a supplementary payment from his/her former employer. To benefit from this system, the employee must have been dismissed by the employer and – once again – must meet certain age and career conditions, which have been hardened over the years to discourage appeals to this system.

Moreover, the Belgian social security system provides for a survivor's pension for the spouse of a retired employee who has deceased. The surviving spouse must be a minimum of 48 years and 6 months if the husband passes away in 2022. This age will be gradually increased to 50 years in 2025 and to 55 in 2030 (every year, another six months is added to the age condition). Yet, in some circumstances, there is no age threshold (when the spouse has a dependent child or has a degree of work incapacity of at least 66%). To be eligible for a survivor's pension, the spouse must not remarry.

Apart from the social security benefits listed above (the 'first pillar'), many employees are entitled to additional pension insurance (the 'second pillar') paid by the employer as part of their salary package. These so-called extra-legal pension plans are either set up under the form of a group insurance contract or as a pension fund (*see* section 12).

Some people also add to these two pillars a private pension insurance scheme (the 'third pillar').

11.3.   VACATION AND HOLIDAY PAYMENTS ON TERMINATION

The number of days of annual leave to which an employee is entitled in a given year is, in principle, determined in proportion to the number of days worked (and deemed to have worked, e.g., where the employee was on maternity leave or sick leave) during the preceding calendar year, referred to as the 'holiday reference year'.

Generally, for a full holiday reference year, employees have the right to between twenty and twenty-four days of annual leave, depending on whether their working regime includes five or six working days per week. This is the statutory minimum, which can be extended by CBAs or by additional days in the employment contract.

Employees are entitled to both single and double holiday pay. A distinction needs to be made between blue- and white-collar employees.

For blue-collar employees, holiday pay is paid through the social security system. It amounts to 15.38% of the gross annual salary, rounded up to 108%. This percentage corresponds to two times four weeks of salary (single and double holiday pay). Both single and double holiday pay are paid when the blue-collar employee takes his/her main holiday, but at the earliest on 2 May.

White-collar employees remain entitled to their normal salary (single holiday pay) during their annual leave. On top of that, they are also entitled to double holiday pay, which amounts to 92% of their gross monthly salary and which is paid when the employee takes his/her main holiday. Contrary to blue-collar employees, holiday pay for white-collar employees is paid by the employer directly to the employee.

As of April 2012, employees who are starting their careers or who are restarting their activities after a long time off are entitled to holidays after an introductory period of three months so that they have the possibility to benefit from four weeks of holiday over the period of one year. The employee will receive holiday pay that is equal to his/her regular salary. The holiday pay will be financed through a deduction from the double holiday pay of the next year.

White-collar employees whose employment contracts are terminated are also entitled to departure holiday pay. In this case, the employer must pay the holiday pay in advance. The departure holiday pay amounts to 15.34% of the salary of the current year and 15.34% of the salary of the holiday reference year, prorated in the function of the number of holidays yet to be taken.

In addition to annual holidays, employees are also entitled to remuneration for ten official Public Holidays. If a Public Holiday falls on a Sunday or on a day on which the employee does not usually work, the employer must grant a replacement day.

11.4. LEAVES OF ABSENCE

11.4.1. Personal Leave

Employees have the right to be temporarily absent (also called 'short leave') from work without salary loss on the occasion of:

- certain family events (marriage, funeral, childbirth, adoption, holy communion, non-confessional youth celebration, etc.);
- for meeting civil duties (jury service, participation in the electoral process, etc.);
- appearance before a court;
- in 2021, a new short leave was introduced for the vaccination against COVID-19.

The reasons for such short leave periods, as well as the duration of the allowed time off (the day of the event, up to a couple of days) for each absence, are provided for in a Royal Decree of 1963. Yet, more favourable provisions may be determined at an industry or company level.

11.4.2. Leave Because of Compelling Reasons

The employee has the right to take leave because of compelling reasons. Compelling reason means any unforeseeable event, independent of the work, which requires the urgent and necessary intervention of the employee, and this insofar as the execution of the employment contract makes this intervention impossible. Examples of compelling reasons are illness, accident or hospitalization of a person living with the employee or damage to the employee's home caused by fire or natural disaster.

The employee must notify the employer in advance and can only take leave as long as is necessary to tend to the emergency and with a maximum of ten days per calendar year (for a full-time employee). This leave is not compensated by the employer (unless agreed otherwise, e.g., in a CBA), nor by the State.

11.4.3. Medical or Sick Leave

In case of illness or a private accident, the white-collar employee continues to receive his/her normal salary during a period of thirty calendar days, while the blue-collar employee continues to receive his/her normal salary during a period of seven calendar days. This is the so-called guaranteed salary.

Before 2014, the first day of sick leave (*carensdag – jour de carence*) was not paid for blue-collar employees; however, this was found to be discriminatory by the Constitutional Court and was abolished with the entry into force of the Unified Employment Status Act.

To be entitled to the guaranteed salary, the employee needs to comply with some legal obligations, which includes, among other things, immediately informing his/her employer of his/her incapacity to work and presenting a medical certificate. The government is planning to prohibit employers from requesting a medical certificate during the first day of absence due to illness, however, this legislation is still in the making. Moreover, the employer may call upon an independent medical officer (the 'controlling officer') to verify an employee's incapacity for work.

During the first year of incapacity following the period covered by the guaranteed salary, the employee will receive sickness benefits from the Health Insurance Fund (*ziekenfonds – mutuelle*). These benefits will be equal to 60% of the employee's gross capped remuneration.

As of the second year, the employee will be entitled to invalidity benefits if the Medical Board for Invalidity of the National Sickness and Invalidity Insurance has confirmed the invalidity (the level of incapacity for work must be at least 66%). These invalidity benefits amount to 65% (for an employee with at least one dependent), 55% (for a single employee) or 40% (for a cohabiting employee without dependents) of the employee's gross capped remuneration.

The Health Insurance Fund also reimburses numerous medical and pharmaceutical costs.

The Royal Decree of 28 October 2016 amended the Royal Decree of 28 May 2003 (now included in the Codex on Well-being at Work) pertaining to the surveillance of employee's health so that a tailor-made reintegration path has been set in place for long-term sick employees. The reintegration procedure tries to let them progress more easily towards an adapted job or another temporary or permanent job. If reintegration is not possible and provided that the reintegration path has been followed, the employer will have the right to end the employment contract for the reason of medical force majeure, without the obligation to pay an indemnity in lieu of notice.

11.4.4.   Bereavement Leave

In case of death of certain family members of the employee or his/her spouse, the employee will be entitled to one, three or ten days of paid leave, depending on the degree of kinship and whether or not the deceased lived under the same roof as the employee. In 2021, the maximum of three days was extend to ten for the death of a spouse or of a cohabitant partner, the death of the own child or of child of a spouse or of a cohabitant partner or the death of a foster child which was under the foster care of the employee for a long period.

11.4.5.   Family Leave

Provided that certain conditions with regard to seniority within the undertaking and minimum employment are met, an employee can resort to the so-called system of 'time credit with motif' if he/she wishes to:

- take care of his/her child until the age of 8;
- provide palliative care;
- provide care to a family member who is seriously ill;
- provide care to his/her disabled child until the age of 21;
- provide care to his/her child who is seriously ill and is part of the household.

This career break system enables employees to suspend their employment contract completely (full break) or to reduce their working hours by half or one-fifth for a maximum period of fifty-one months. During this period, they will receive a lump sum monthly allowance from the National

Unemployment Office (*RVA – ONEM*) on top of their reduced salary. For a full-time time credit, this lump sum allowance amounts to EUR 552.55 gross in case the employee has less than five years of seniority within the undertaking, or to EUR 644.64 gross in case the employee has at least five years of seniority with the employer (figures for 2022).

For a full break or a reduction of working time to part-time employment, a CBA needs to be entered into at either an industry or company level.

Besides time credit, the Belgian labour law system also provides for other leave schemes (*thematische verloven – congés thématiques*) for employees wanting to take care of their family. While not an exhaustive list, these other leave schemes include:

– parental leave: complete suspension of the employment contract for three months, half-time reduction of working time during six months, reduction by one-fifth during a period of fifteen months or a reduction of one-tenth during a period of forty months to take care of a child up to the age of 12;[22]
– palliative care;
– adoption leave;
– leave for foster parents.

11.4.6. Pregnancy Leave

During an employee's period of pregnancy, the employee has a right to be absent from her work to attend medical examinations if the examinations cannot take place outside the employee's normal working hours. The employee will retain her normal wage during these absences if she informs her employer before each absence. The employee will need to provide a medical certificate in case the Work Rules or a CBA require this or upon request of the employer.

Each employer has to make sure that a pregnant employee is not exposed to hazardous work or substances. In this respect, the employer has to arrange an appointment with the occupational physician, who will determine whether the pregnant employee should be:

– removed partially from her job, by assigning another function or less working hours, or by providing other working conditions;
– removed entirely from her job if the above is not possible.

If the removal entails a loss of salary, an allocation amounting to 60% of the gross income for the concerned hours will be issued. This allocation

---

22. During the COVID-19 pandemic, a temporary new system for parental leave was created for parents whose children's schools would close due to an outbreak of the coronavirus.

amounts to 78.237% of the gross income during the period of pregnancy in case of entire removal from the employee's function.

11.4.7. Maternity Leave

Women may take up to fifteen weeks of maternity leave (with a possible extension of two weeks in case of multiple births). At least nine weeks must be taken after the birth, and at least one week must be taken before the expected date of birth.

Women receive maternity benefits while on maternity leave. The benefit paid by the social security system is equal to 82% of the employee's salary for the first thirty days and then drops to 75% of her salary (which will be capped). During this period, the employer is not obliged to make any payments to the employee.

Following the birth of a child, the father or co-parent has a right to fifteen days of birth leave (before 2021, this was called paternity leave), twelve of which will be paid for by the social security system at 82% of the employee's ceiled salary. This leave must be taken within four months after the birth. As of 1 January 2023, the birth leave will be extended to twenty days.

11.4.8. Injury at Work

An accident at work is defined as 'any accident that happens to an employee during the course and by the fact of the performance of his/her employment contract and which causes an injury'.

All employees, including apprentices/trainees and domestic workers, are insured against accidents at work or on the way to and from work.

It is incumbent on every employer to enter into an insurance contract for occupational accidents with a recognized insurance company.

In case the employer fails to do so, it:

– risks criminal or administrative sanctions;
– is obliged to pay contributions to the Occupational Accidents Fund by way of a fine;
– will have to reimburse all the indemnities that are paid out by the fund to the employer's employees.

During a period of temporary total incapacity, the victim of an accident at work will receive 90% of his/her average daily pay. A cash benefit is also paid for temporary partial incapacity. If the victim returns to partial employment, he or she will receive benefits equal to the difference between the pay received before the accident and that received after returning to work.

If the injury continues to exist but remains stable, it has 'consolidated', and the temporary incapacity becomes permanent. After 'consolidation', an annual allowance is paid, which can be re-examined during the first three years of consolidation. At the end of these three years, the allowance is converted into a life annuity.

11.5. CHECKLIST OF DOS AND DON'TS

- The granting of additional insurances on top of the social security benefits can make a remuneration package more attractive to applicants and can help to win over the best candidates.
- A thorough follow-up of employees who are ill frequently (and/or long-term) is highly recommended. A controlling officer can be sent to the domicile or place of residence of the employee to ascertain the illness. A time range of four consecutive hours can be included within a CBA or within the Work Rules, during which the absent employee must be available for an examination by the controlling officer at his/her domicile or place of residence. In case of absence during this time slot, the employee will lose his/her right to the guaranteed salary for the days preceding the examination.
- In case of frequent and/or long-term illnesses, it is advisable to send letters to the employee arguing that his/her absences disrupt the good functioning of the service in order to build up a possible dismissal case.

12. WORKERS' COMPENSATION

12.1. OVERVIEW

Belgian law does not fix gross salary levels. In principle, minimum wages are fixed per sector of industry in CBAs; however, these minimum wages may not be lower than the guaranteed average minimum monthly pay, fixed by national CBA (*see* sections 10.1 and 10.2).

For most white-collar employees, especially those at a senior or management level, the salaries are negotiated individually and are higher than the minimum wages of the sector of the industry.

In addition to their monthly gross salary, white-collar employees are entitled to single and double holiday pay (*see* section 11.3). Moreover, in most sectors of industry, the payment of an end-of-year premium of one month is mandatory (*see* section 10.1).

Some employers also grant their employees additional or non-statutory fringe benefits. These vary widely and may be laid down in the provisions of company CBAs, or in the individual employment agreement.

Granting bonuses to employees is common. The bonus terms and conditions are freely determined by the employer or by the parties. The bonus is part of the remuneration and is subject to social security contributions and income tax. On top of the bonus, the employer also has to compensate for the holiday pay related to this bonus.

On the gross salary, the employer pays his own social security contributions and withholds the employee's social security contributions, as well as withholding taxes. Given the complexity of the social security and tax calculations, most employers rely on a payroll agency to handle their payroll administration.

12.2.   FRINGE BENEFITS

12.2.1.   Examples of Fringe Benefits

– *Meal vouchers.* Meal vouchers are a very popular benefit as they are, in principle, exempt from taxation and social security contributions.
– The maximum total value of an exempted meal voucher is set at EUR 8 per day, which is actually worked, of which the employee must pay a personal contribution of at least EUR 1.09.
– *Eco-vouchers.* Employers can award their employers eco-vouchers with which they can buy eco-friendly goods (e.g., eco-friendly household electronics, bikes, plants, …). In some sectors, it is mandatory to give eco-vouchers (laid down in a CBA). Eco-vouchers are exempt from taxation and social security contributions until a value of EUR 250/year.
– *Extra-legal pension schemes.* It is very common in Belgium that an employer funds an extra-legal pension scheme via a group insurance scheme or a pension fund to grant the employees a supplement to their statutory pension.

It is a very attractive fringe benefit, as the employer's contributions to the pension scheme (the premiums) are exempt from the normal social security contributions and taxation. As a consequence, these premiums are only subject to an employer's social security contribution, which is currently less than 30% of the normal social security contributions on a cash salary. Furthermore, the pension is taxed at a favourable tax rate. There are, however, strict non-discrimination rules that have to be complied with when introducing such a pension scheme:

- *A mobile phone and voice (and data) subscription.* If the employees are allowed to use their professional phone and subscription for private purposes at the employer's expense, this benefit in kind will be subject to income taxes and social security contributions.
- *A company car and fuel card.* If a company car may also be used for commuting to the normal workplace or for any other private purposes, this benefit in kind is subject to income taxes. This benefit is exempt from normal social security contributions, but it is subject to a special employer's social security contribution. The value of the benefit in kind depends on the official price of the car, the type of fuel and the CO_2 emission of the car. Cars that pollute less will be valued at a lower benefit in kind.
- A *mobility budget.* When an employer introduces a mobility budget in the company, employees who have (a right to) a company car can exchange this for a mobility budget. The mobility budget can be spent on three pillars: (1) an eco-friendly car (electric/hybrid); (2) endurable ways of transport (e.g., bikes, shared cars and public transport) and housing costs; (3) the left-over budget in cash. The first and second pillars are exempted from social security contributions. Except for the private benefit of the eco-friendly car, the mobility budget is exempted from income taxes.
- *Hospitalization insurance.* The premium paid for such an insurance by the employer are exempted from social security contributions and taxes.

12.2.2. Fringe Benefits Are Considered to be Part of the Remuneration

Fringe benefits are considered to be part of the remuneration. As a consequence, an employer cannot revoke existing fringe benefits without the consent of the employees.

This implies that these benefits are also taken into account for the calculation of the indemnity in lieu of notice in case of dismissal (*see* section 5).

12.3. CHECKLIST OF DOS AND DON'TS

- Draft the bonus plans in the correct language (Dutch, French or German, depending on the location of the operational unit of the company). All clauses, which are not drafted in the correct language, may be considered null and void. Such nullity may, however, never deprive the employee of his/her rights.

- If the employer does not want the bonus to be considered as an acquired right that will continue in the future, a clause in the employment contract should indicate that the bonus could be revoked at any time.
- Make sure that every benefit in kind is properly declared on the employee's payslip.
- Always check any obligations laid down in CBAs at an industry level.

13. COMPANY'S OBLIGATION TO PROVIDE A SAFE AND HEALTHY WORKPLACE

13.1. OVERVIEW OF SAFETY AND ENVIRONMENTAL ACTS AND REGULATIONS

The basic regulation on health and safety in Belgium is the Act of 4 August 1996 on the well-being of employees during the performance of their work ('Well-Being Act').

This Act creates a framework in the execution of which different Royal Decrees have been adopted in order to apply the principles of the Well-Being Act. These Royal Decrees have been codified in the Well-Being Code of 2 June 2017, which entered into force on 12 June 2017.

Well-being at work covers measures related to:

- security at work;
- protection of the employee's health at work;
- psychosocial aspects;
- ergonomics;
- hygiene at work;
- embellishment of workplaces;
- environmental measures linked to the previous points.

The well-being legislation defines goals but not the means to achieve these goals. This grants flexibility to the employer.

The legislation on health and safety also provides for the involvement of different key actors. Every employer is obliged to establish an 'Internal Service for Prevention and Protection at Work' (the 'Internal Service'). This body assists the employer, the members of the hierarchical line and the employees with implementing the legal and regulatory provisions regarding the well-being of the employees and all prevention measures and activities. For this purpose, every employer has at least one 'Prevention Advisor', competent for safety at work (the 'Safety Prevention Advisor'), an employee of the undertaking and connected to an Internal Service. In companies employing less than twenty employees, it is the employer that may exercise the function of Safety Prevention Advisor. The higher the risk of the company (based on the number of employees and the nature of the activities), the more tasks will be executed by the Internal Service; the lower the risk of the company, the less tasks will weigh upon the Internal Service and the more responsibilities can be outsourced to a so-called External Service for Prevention and Protection at Work (the 'External Service'), with whom the employer collaborates. External Services must be duly authorized by the authorities.

Other specialized Prevention Advisors intervene in matters related to psychosocial risks at work (the 'Prevention Advisor-Psychosocial Risks') or occupational medicine (the 'Prevention Advisor-Occupational Physician'). These Prevention Advisors can be internal or external, depending on the size of the company. An external Prevention Advisor is an employee of an External Service.

A 'Committee for Prevention and Protection at Work' (hereinafter 'Health and Safety Committee') is to be set up in all undertakings that usually employ an average of fifty employees. This body's main assignment is to contribute actively to everything that is undertaken to promote the employees' well-being in the execution of their work.

13.2. REQUIREMENTS

The employer has to take the necessary measures to promote the well-being of the employees during the performance of their work (*see* section 13.3).

The employee has to take care, as much as possible, of his/her own health and security and that of the other persons concerned by his/her acts or omissions at work, in accordance with his/her education and the employer's instructions (*see* section 13.4).

13.3. OBLIGATIONS OF THE EMPLOYER

The Well-Being Act does not directly provide rights for the employees but includes obligations for the employer, which correspondingly generates rights for the employees.

To meet its general obligation (*see* section 13.2), the employer needs to apply, among others, the following general prevention action principles:

- avoid risks, evaluate the risks which cannot be avoided and combat such risks at the source;
- give collective protective measures priority over individual protective measures;

- adapt the work to the individual, especially as regards to the design of workplaces, the choice of work equipment and the choice of working and production methods, with a view, in particular, to alleviate monotonous work and work at predetermined work rates and to reduce their effect on health;
- limit risks as much as possible, taking technical progress into account;
- limit the risk of serious injury by taking material measures and giving them priority over any other measures;
- inform the employee on the nature of his/her work, on the associated residual risks and on the measures aimed at preventing or limiting these hazards when commencing employment and whenever necessary for protecting well-being;
- give appropriate instructions to the employees and establish guidelines to reasonably guarantee compliance with these instructions;
- provide or ascertain the existence of appropriate safety and health signs at work.

The employer determines the means and the way to carry out the well-being policy as well as the competencies and responsibilities of the persons in charge of applying the well-being policy.

Furthermore, the employer is required to draw up a number of mandatory documents pertaining to health and safety rules. The most important ones are as follows:

- *A Global Prevention Plan.* In this five-year plan, the results of the company's risk analysis and the prevention activities to be developed and adopted with regard to safety and health need to be programmed, taking into account the size of the company and the nature of the risks attached to the activities of the company.
- *Yearly Action Plan.* This plan works out the Global Prevention Plan on a yearly basis.
- *Yearly report* on the activities of the *Internal Service.*

For a complete overview of these mandatory documents, *see* section 10.9.

The well-being rules played an important role during the COVID-19 pandemic as the employer has to ensure the health and safety of his employees. At the beginning of the crisis, this was guaranteed by mandatory closure, mandatory telework or social distancing measures, and the obligation for employers to take the necessary measures to prevent the spread of the virus at the workplace. The government provided a Generic Guide with preventive measures, which were further specified with sector-specific guidelines (published by the Joint Committees). The Prevention Advisor or the prevention service (internal or external) and the

Health and Safety Committee play an important role in the setup and the implementation of the preventive measures.

13.4.   OBLIGATIONS OF THE EMPLOYEE

To meet his/her general obligation (*see* section 13.2), the employee needs to:

− correctly use the machinery, apparatus, tools, dangerous substances, transport equipment, and other means of production;
− correctly use the personal protective equipment supplied to him/her and, after use, return it to its proper place;
− refrain from arbitrarily disconnecting, changing or moving safety devices fitted, e.g., to machinery, apparatus, tools, plant and buildings and use such safety devices correctly;
− immediately inform the employer and the Internal Service of any work situation he/she has reasonable grounds for considering as representing a serious and immediate danger to safety and health and of any shortcomings in the protection arrangement;
− cooperate with the employer and the Internal Service, as long as necessary to enable any tasks or requirements imposed by the competent authority to protect the well-being of the employees at work;
− cooperate with the employer and the Internal Service, for as long as may be necessary to enable the employer to ensure that the working environment and working conditions are safe and pose no risk to safety and health within their field of activity;
− contribute positively to the prevention policy that is brought about within the context of the protection of employees against violence, bullying or sexual harassment at work, refrain from any act of violence, bullying or sexual harassment at work and refrain from any unlawful use of the procedures.

13.5.   SPECIFIC STANDARDS

Specific standards apply with regard to a variety of situations, such as, among others:

− *Companies with certain high-risk activities*: where substantial amounts of *asbestos* may be released, the employer is obliged to call in an authorized company to carry out demolition or disposal work.
− *Undertakings sharing the same workplace or operating at adjoining or neighbouring workplaces*: they need to cooperate in implementing the

measures regarding the well-being of the employees, coordinate their actions and provide one another with necessary information.

- *Work executed by outside undertakings:* the employer in whose facilities work is being performed by *contractors* and, where applicable, *subcontractors*, will need to comply with a number of obligations (e.g., provide the contractors with the necessary information with regard to health and safety, ascertain that the employees of the (sub)contractors have received appropriate training, conclude an agreement with every contractor including that the contractor undertakes to meet his/her obligations and to make his/her subcontractors meet the obligations regarding the employees' well-being and that if the contractor fails to meet these obligations, the employer in whose facility the work is executed, can, at the expense of the contractor, take the necessary measures itself, etc.). The contractors and, where applicable, the subcontractors have the same obligations towards their subcontractors as the employer has towards the contractors.

- *Temporary or mobile construction sites:* several obligations apply to activities of building or civil engineering works. For instance, the client or the project supervisor responsible for the design has an obligation to appoint a coordinator for safety and health matters at the project preparation stage for any construction site on which more than one contractor is present. Moreover, the presence of each natural person on the site must be registered by means of an electronic presence recording system, by using any other automatic recording mode or by putting it at the disposal of his or her subcontractors.

13.6. INJURY OR ACCIDENT AT WORK

13.6.1. General Considerations

Under Belgian legislation, an accident at work (or 'occupational accident') is an accident of an employee during and due to the performance of the employment contract that causes a lesion. Injury at work is included in this concept. An accident that occurs out of the performance of the employment contract, but that is caused by a third party because the employment contract is also covered. Likewise, an accident that occurs on the normal way to and from the workplace is also considered an occupational accident.

The employer must take several measures to manage, examine and prevent the repetition of occupational accidents.

13.6.2. Severe Occupational Accidents

After every severe occupational accident (e.g., an occupational accident that led to death), the employer of the victim sees to it that the accident is immediately investigated by its competent prevention service and that it submits a circumstantial report to the Social Inspectorate within ten days following the accident.

13.6.3. Measures to Be Taken with Regard to All Occupational Accidents

The employer ensures that the Internal Service, which is charged with this assignment, draws up an occupational accident index card for every accident that has caused at least four days of occupational disability. The notice form for the occupational accident intended for the competent social insurance system may replace the occupational accident index card, provided that the data required to draw up the index card is filled in on the notice form.

In cases where the Internal Service that has filled in the occupational accident index card or the notice form of the occupational accident is not responsible for the medical supervision of the employees, the employer sends a copy or a printout of the index card or the notice form to the section responsible for medical supervision of its External Service.

The employer keeps the occupational accident index cards, copies or printouts of the forms on which the occupational accidents were reported for at least ten years.

13.7. WORKPLACE VIOLENCE

Under Belgian law, workplace violence is a part of the broader concept of 'psychosocial risk', which covers any potential psychological damage, potentially accompanied by physical damage, linked to work in its widest sense (e.g., organization of work, working conditions, interpersonal relationships), on which the employer has an influence and which objectively involves a danger. Violence, moral or sexual harassment, stress and an excessive workload are types of psychosocial risks.

Management of psychosocial risks revolves around three key phases: prevention, internal procedure and external remedies.

13.7.1.   Prevention

Risk analyses constitute the keystones of the prevention system. Two types of analysis exist: (i) a general analysis, as an integral part of the overall management of risks that the employer is obliged to implement; and (ii) a specific analysis relating to an individual work situation holding a danger.

The employer is only obliged to carry out a specific risk analysis when it is asked to do so by a member of the hierarchical line or when at least one-third of the representatives of the employees in the Health and Safety Committee requires the employer to do so.

13.7.2.   Internal Procedure

(1) An employee who is deemed to be a victim of a psychosocial risk may address his/her employer, a member of the hierarchical line, a member of the Health and Safety Committee or a Trade Union Delegate directly:

(a) he/she may also resort to the internal procedure, consisting of two phases:– A compulsory preliminary phase prior to any request, during which the Confidential Counsellor (*vertrouwenspersoon – personne de confiance*) or the Prevention Advisor listens to the employee and advises him/her on the available procedures; and

(b) upon the employee's choice:

(i) an informal request for psychosocial intervention, consisting of interviews, conciliations and/or intervention from an outside party within the undertaking; or

(ii) a formal request for psychosocial intervention, with a special feature in case of acts of violence or moral or sexual harassment.

(2) Besides an individual risk, the application for a formal intervention may also address a collective risk. This means that psychosocial risk affects several employees and has an impact on the work organization.

13.7.3.   External Remedies

(1) In the case where the employer fails to react to the employee's request for intervention or decides that no action is required, or if the employee is of the opinion that the measures taken are inappropriate, the employee may apply to several institutions (i.e., the Inspectorate

well-being at work, the Public Prosecutor, the Labour or Criminal Court).

(2) Notwithstanding the actual injury, the employee who is the victim of violence or sexual or moral harassment may also claim a lump sum compensation for his/her damage from the perpetrator before the Labour Court. Such a lump sum will amount to:

(a) three months of gross remuneration (capped at a reference remuneration of EUR 44,817.89 per year); or

(b) six months of gross remuneration (capped at a reference remuneration of 44,817.89 per year) if:

(i) the behaviour is related to a statutory criterion of discrimination;

(ii) the perpetrator is in a position of authority over the victim; or

(iii) the gravity of the facts justifies it.

(3) Since the jurisdiction of the Labour Courts covers all psychosocial risks at work, the employee may also attempt to hold the employer or the perpetrator liable for facts that are not constitutive of violence or harassment (e.g., stress, burnout). In this case, the law does not provide for lump sum compensation, and the employee must prove his/her actual damage.

(4) If the judge establishes that the employee has addressed the court without first having gone through the internal procedure in the company, he/she may order the employee to undertake this procedure first. The judge will then suspend the judicial proceedings awaiting the outcome of the internal procedure.

The law protects the employee who introduced a formal request concerning violence or moral or sexual harassment, as well as witnesses to the procedure, against dismissal or any other detrimental measures.

The employer has to prove that the termination or the detrimental measure is not linked to the formal request for intervention based on acts of violence or moral or sexual harassment. If the employer fails to do so, the employee will be able to claim:

- a lump sum amount of six months of pay (without cap); or
- compensation for the actual harm suffered.

13.8. FINES AND PENALTIES

The Social Penal Code distinguishes between four categories of sanctions, depending on the gravity of the violation. The lightest violations (level 1) are de-penalized and can only lead to administrative fines. Violations of moderate gravity (level 2) and serious violations (level 3) can be punished either by an administrative fine or by a penal fine. Only for the most serious violations (level 4) is imprisonment possible.

The violations related to violence or moral or sexual harassment at work are listed in Articles 119 through 122 of the Social Penal Code. In summary, the perpetrator of acts of violence or harassment is punished with a level 4 sanction, and the employer who does not respect certain legal obligations in this respect is punished with a sanction ranging from level 1 to level 4, depending on the nature of the violation.

The other infringements on health and safety are listed in Articles 123 through 133 of the Social Penal Code. Most of these infringements are punished with a level 3 sanction. If the violation causes damage to the employee's health or constitutes an occupational accident, the violation will be punishable with a level 4 sanction.

If the violation leads to death or injuries, Article 418 of the Criminal Code related to involuntary manslaughter and injuries will also apply.

13.9. CHECKLISTS OF DOS AND DON'TS

– Undertake clear risk analysis and provide sufficient resources to the Prevention Advisor, the Internal or External Service and other actors to ensure that the risks can be reduced and the lessons from a past occupational accident are learned.
– Draft a delegation policy, which places the responsibilities on the persons that have the power to make decisions. Most of the time, the final responsibility will fall on persons at a director level, as the delegate must have the necessary competence, authority and means to carry out his/her tasks.
– Inform your employees about the risks, repeat the information and check that the security instructions are complied with.
– Make sure that all procedures regarding psychosocial risks at work, including violence and moral or sexual harassment, as well as the contact details of the Prevention Advisor and the Confidential Counsellor, are specified in the Work Rules.

14. IMMIGRATION, SECONDMENT AND FOREIGN ASSIGNMENT

14.1. OVERVIEW OF LAWS CONTROLLING IMMIGRATION

European treaties provide for the free movement of persons within the EEA and Switzerland. Thus, employees who are citizens of one EEA Member State or Switzerland are, in principle, free to work in another Member State without a work permit.

In principle, every non-EEA national working in Belgium must be in possession of a work permit, although some categories of employees are exempt from this requirement.

14.1.1. Visa and Residence Permit

In case of a short stay in Belgium (less than ninety days within any given period of six months), the question of whether or not a visa is required for entering Belgium will depend on the foreign employee's nationality. If the employee is an EEA or Swiss national, no visa is required. If the employee is a non-EEA national, a visa is, in principle, required.

In case non-EEA nationals are staying in Belgium for more than ninety days within any given period of six months, they must be in possession of a type-D visa to enter the country and are required to obtain a Belgian residence permit.

In case EEA or Swiss nationals are staying in Belgium for more than ninety days within any given period of six months, no visa is required, but a residence permit will have to be obtained.

14.1.2. Single Permit: Work and Residence Permit

In principle, every non-EEA national working in Belgium must be in possession of a work permit, although some categories of workers are exempt from this requirement. In 2019, Belgium introduced the single permit, which combines the work permit and residence permit into one single procedure. The single permit has to be applied for in Belgium by the employer or an agent, and the employer must obtain prior authorization to employ that person. The necessary documents have to be sent to the competent department of the Region where the worker is posted (where he will carry out his work). These are as follows:

– Brussels Capital Region:

Brussels Economy and Employment
Direction de la Migration économique
Place Saint-Lazare 2, 1035 Brussels
Tel.: +32 (0)2 204 13 99
Website:
http://werk-economie-emploi.brussels/en/single-permit-work-permit
- Flanders:
  Department Werk en Sociale Economie Vlaanderen, Team
  Arbeidskaarten
  Boulevard du Roi Albert II 35, box 20, 1030 Brussels
  Tel.: +32 (0)2 553 43 00
  E-mail: arbeidskaart@vlaanderen.be
  Website:
  www.vlaanderen.be/gecombineerde-vergunning-van-bepaalde-duur
  (NL)
- Wallonia:
  Service public de Wallonie, Direction opérationnelle Economie, Emploi
  et Recherche, Département de l'Emploi et des Permis de Travail
  Place de Wallonie, 1, 5100 Jambes
  Tel.: +32 (0)81 33 43 92 – +32 (0)81 33 43 38
  E-mail: permisdetravail.entreprises@spw.wallonie.be
  Website:
  https://emploi.wallonie.be/en/home/travailleurs-etrangers/permis-de-travail.html

Access to the single permit procedure is restricted to certain categories of workers, which are enshrined in the regional regulations. There is a residuary category for workers that succeed in a labour market test (which is very strict): in this case, the employer needs to demonstrate that he cannot find the profile he is looking for on the Belgian labour market. However, most important and common are the categories of highly skilled workers and managerial employees, which means the employee has to fulfil certain conditions of higher education degrees and higher wages, or they have to take up certain leading functions within the company. As said, the specific conditions to be fulfilled and the necessary documents which have to be submitted are laid down in the legislation of the Regions, but in general, the following documents will be necessary for posting non-EEA workers:

- Copy of the passport of the worker.
- Copy of the degree(s) of the worker.
- Recent criminal records of the worker.
- Recent medical certificate of the worker.
- Employment contract between the posting company and the worker.
- Proof of insurance coverage.

– Proof of the payment of the administrative fees.
– Power of attorney for the agent of the foreign employer.

These documents have to be submitted together with the regional application form (signed by the employer and the employee). These application forms will be only in Dutch or French. Submitting English documents is allowed, but documents in other languages should be translated by an official translator.

The regional Department of Work will first check whether the application is complete. The department will notify the employer within ten to fifteen days if the application is admissible. If not, the employer has fifteen days to submit the missing information or documents. If the application is complete, the Department of Work will send the application to the Federal Foreigners Office. Then the Department of Work and the Foreigners Office have a maximum of four months (after the decision of admissibility) to decide upon respectively the permission to work and stay on the Belgian territory. In practice, the term to obtain a single permit is shorter than four months, depending on the workload of the competent administration and the complexity of the situation. If both decisions are positive, the Foreigners Office will notify the employer and the employee, and it will send the necessary visa to the diplomatic post or to the community where the employee is staying.

If the Foreigners Office's decision is negative, an appeal is possible before the Foreigners' Litigation Council (administrative court). If the decision of the Department of Work is negative, an appeal is possible before the competent regional minister of work. An ultimate appeal in both cases is possible before the Council of State.

Some categories of non-EEA citizens are exempt from obtaining a single permit. For example, the spouse of Belgian or EEA nationals (under certain conditions).

14.1.3.   LIMOSA Declaration

Finally, it should be stressed that all foreign employees coming to work in Belgium on a temporary basis must be reported to the Belgian social security authority, i.e., the National Social Security Office (*RSZ – ONSS*), prior to the start of their activities. This declaration is called 'LIMOSA' and can be done electronically via https://www.international.socialsecurity.be/working_in_belgium/en/limosa.html. There are, however, a number of exemptions, mainly depending on the nature and the duration of the temporary activities in Belgium.

The LIMOSA tracking system is aimed at monitoring foreign workers presence in Belgium and allows the local authorities to verify the compliance of foreign companies who post workers to Belgium with a number of core rules pertaining, *inter alia*, to work permit, minimum wages, working time, rest periods, etc.

As a result of filing the LIMOSA declaration, the employer will be exempt from the obligation to draw up the so-called social documents for a period of twelve months. After the initial twelve-month period, the employer will need to draw up these documents, which mainly include the personnel register, the Work Rules (*arbeidsreglement – règlement de travail*), and the individual payroll accounts (payslips and overview of the annual earnings).

14.2. Recruiting, Screening and Hiring Process

The process of recruiting foreign employees (i.e., non-EEA nationals) to work in Belgium is one that should be well planned and carefully executed in order to maximize the prospects of a successful outcome.

Step one is to determine whether the job concerned falls within the scope of a category of allowed worker, which is subject to an exemption from the labour market test or qualifies as a 'bottleneck occupation' (i.e., the job concerns an occupation for which there is a lack of staff in Belgium; such shortfall occupations are officially listed and annually adapted to the labour market situation). Once qualified candidates have been selected, it should be verified whether they personally benefit from any exemption.

If a work permit is necessary, an application for such work permit should be made in due course, and a written employment contract (conditional upon the delivery of a work permit) should be entered into (in certain cases, the contract must include some mandatory provisions).

14.3. The Obligation of Employer to Enforce Immigration Laws

An employer is legally obliged to verify whether its foreign employees have a valid residence permit and keep a copy thereof that can be presented to the inspection services. The employer is liable for the repatriation and the accommodation costs of the foreign employee (and his/her family) if he/she has no valid residence permit.

An employer must ensure that its foreign employees have the relevant (single) permit in order to legally work in Belgium and is obliged to declare the entering into service and the departure of its employees (Dimona – *LIMOSA* declaration).

14.4.   FINES AND PENALTIES

An employer employing a foreign employee without a valid residence permit can be imprisoned (from six months to three years) and/or fined up to EUR 48,000 per employee concerned. Moreover, a court can order the closure of the company for a duration ranging from one month to three years. Infringement of the rules relating to work permits is criminally sanctioned with a fine of up to EUR 8,000 per employee concerned.

14.5.   SECONDMENT/FOREIGN ASSIGNMENT

When employing personnel in Belgium (even temporarily), a foreign employer is required to respect, at a minimum, the labour, salary, and employment conditions laid down in Belgian statutory provisions that are criminally sanctioned (which is the vast majority) or in CBAs that have generally been declared binding by Royal Decree.

Employees working in Belgium are, in principle, covered by the Belgian social security system. However, depending on the employee's nationality (EEA + Switzerland or not), an exception may apply if the employee is seconded to Belgium, in which case the employee remains covered by his/her home social security system, provided that the secondment does not exceed a certain duration (in principle two years and a maximum of up to five years in certain cases). A secondment requires that a link of subordination remains to exist between the employee and his/her foreign employer. A certificate of coverage (E-101 or A1-declaration) must be issued by the 'sending' EU Member State as proof that the employee and the employer are subject to the payment of social security contributions in the foreign country.

If, however, the employee is fully linked to the Belgian place of business (i.e., the hierarchical relation is located in Belgium), the employment will not be regarded as a secondment but rather a transfer. A new local Belgian employment contract will be deemed to have been entered into between parties, and the Belgian social security system will be applicable to their situation.

For non-EEA foreign workers, it is possible that Belgium has concluded a bilateral treaty with the sending state in order to determine the applicable social security system.

Be aware that non-EEA foreign workers will have to apply for a single permit to be able to legally work and stay in Belgium.

14.6.   CHECKLIST OF DOS AND DON'TS

– Implement procedures to only hire foreign employees who have the necessary residence and work permits.
– Note the expiration date of the foreign employees' work permit and apply for a renewal if and when necessary.
– Insert a clause in the employment contract according to which the contract automatically ends when the foreign employee's (residence or work) permits expire and/or according to which the contract only can enter into force after the necessary permits are obtained.

15.   RESTRICTIVE COVENANTS AND PROTECTION OF TRADE SECRETS AND CONFIDENTIAL INFORMATION

15.1.   OVERVIEW

Article 17 of the Employment Contracts Act provides that during the contract and after its termination, the employee must abstain from: (i) obtaining, using or disclosing in an unlawful manner, a trade secret within the meaning of Article I.17/1, 1° of the Code of Economic Law, of which he may become aware in the exercise of his professional activity, as well as to disclose secrets relating to personal or confidential matters, of which he may become aware in the exercise of his professional activity; (ii) performing or cooperating with any act of unfair competition. These two obligations partly result from the duty of good faith, which governs any contract under the rules of Belgian civil law. However, the first obligation was adapted by the recent Act of 30 July 2018 on the protection of trade secrets.

15.2.   THE LAW OF TRADE SECRETS

Trade secrets and, more widely, any confidential information, which the employee may have acquired in the course of his/her employment, are protected by Article 17 of the Employment Contracts Act. Trade secrets are defined by Article I.17/1, 1° of the Code of Economic Law as information meeting the following cumulative conditions: (i) it is secret in the sense that it is not, as a whole or in the precise configuration and assembly of its components, generally known among, or readily accessible to, persons within the circles normally involved in the type of information concerned; (ii) it has commercial value because it is secret; (iii) it has been subject to reasonable measures of confidentiality by the person lawfully in possession of it, with regard to the circumstances of the case.

The communication of trade secrets is sanctioned by Article 309 of the Penal Code, which includes imprisonment for three months to three years and/or a fine ranging from EUR 400 to EUR 16,000. This sanction presupposes that the employee's malicious intent be proven.

Disclosing confidential information may also give rise to dismissal for a serious cause, especially if this disclosure occurs consciously, and the payment of financial compensation if the employer is able to prove that it has suffered damages as a consequence of the non-authorized divulging of information.

With a view to detail the information covered by the duty of confidentiality, a confidentiality agreement is often inserted into employment contracts. This common practice is authorized, provided that the confidentiality agreement does not impose more stringent obligations on the employee than those directly flowing from Article 17 of the Employment Contracts Act (e.g., a confidentiality agreement cannot cover information of a non-confidential nature). The confidentiality agreement may also provide for a lump sum payment in case of violation of its provisions, which would occur after the end of the employment contract, provided that the payment is of a compensatory, as opposed to punitive, nature. This lump sum compensation should not be disproportionate.

15.3. RESTRICTIVE COVENANTS AND NON-COMPETE AGREEMENTS

As a consequence of the principle of good faith, the employee is prohibited from competing with his/her employer during the execution of the employment contract. A non-compete clause, which recalls this prohibition, may validly be inserted into the employment contract without any specific formality or condition.

For a non-compete clause to apply after termination of the employment contract, strict conditions have to be complied with. The clause must be in writing and is valid if the employee's annual gross remuneration exceeds EUR 73,571.00 (except if prohibited by CBA). There are further restrictions on its applicability if the annual gross remuneration does not exceed EUR 73,571.00, as a CBA authorizing it must be entered into at an industry or company level, and the annual gross remuneration must, in any case, exceed EUR 36,785.00 (these amounts, applicable for 2022, are updated annually).

In general, a non-compete clause is valid if it is limited to activities similar to those presently performed by the employee and to a well-defined geographical area limited to the national territory, if the new employer is a competitor, and provided that the clause does not exceed twelve months.

Except for sales representatives, the clause must provide for the payment of an indemnity to the employee equal to at least 50% of the salary corresponding to the duration of the non-compete provision. The clause is not applicable if: (i) the employer terminates the contract during the first six months of employment; (ii) if after the first six months of employment, the employer terminates the employment contract with a notice period or an indemnity in lieu of notice; or (iii) the employee puts an end to the agreement on the basis of a serious breach committed by the employer.

Provided that some specific requirements are met, various deviations from the conditions of the general non-compete clause can be carried through (i.e., the 'special non-compete clause'). This clause may only be used for certain categories of enterprises and for white-collar employees (except sales representatives) with specific functions.

The enterprises concerned have to comply with one of the following conditions:

– they must have an international activity or considerable economic, technical or financial interests in the international markets; or
– they must have their own research department.

In such enterprises, the special non-compete clause may only be applied to those employees whose work allows them to directly or indirectly acquire a practice or knowledge peculiar to the enterprise, which, if used by another entity, could be detrimental.

If these conditions are met, it is possible to deviate from the general non-competition clause insofar as it restricts the geographical application of the non-compete to the national territory and is limited to a maximum period of twelve months. This means that the special non-compete clause can be applicable outside of Belgium (it should enlist the applicable countries or regions). The special non-compete clause may also be applicable when the employment contract is terminated by the employer with a notice period or an indemnity in lieu of notice after the first six months of employment have elapsed, or if the contract is terminated during the first six months of employment, whatever the cause of the termination may be.

15.4.   CHECKLIST OF DOS AND DON'TS

It is advisable for employers to enter into confidentiality agreements with employees, detailing the content of the employee's duty of confidentiality. When doing so, the employer must, however, be careful not to impose more stringent obligations on the employee than those prescribed by law (e.g., non-confidential information). The employer must also avoid setting a lump sum payment for the violation of a confidentiality agreement after the termination of the employment contract at a level that is too high and which might be deemed punitive if challenged in court.

Non-compete clauses may be inserted into employment contracts with a view to preventing competition from employees with a certain salary level after the termination of the employment contract. However, the conditions prescribed by law have to be respected. It is important to note that an employer must renounce the application of the non-compete agreement within fifteen days of the date of the termination of the employment contract if it wishes to avoid paying the lump sum provided for in the non-compete clause.

16. PROTECTION OF WHISTLE-BLOWING CLAIMS

16.1. OVERVIEW

The former Belgian Commission for the Protection of Privacy ('Privacy Commission') (now replaced by the Data Protection Authority) describes 'whistle-blowing' as follows: 'whistleblowing systems are mechanisms that enable individuals to report conduct of a member of their organisation, which in their opinion is contrary to a law or a regulation or to the basic rules established by their organisation'. The implementation of such a system implies taking into account the legitimate interests of all the parties involved (the organization, its staff, the whistle-blower, the person incriminated, third parties, etc.).

There is still no specific Belgian legislation governing whistle-blowing in private employment law. However, the relevant case law is a good indicator of the admitted practices. Although the number of cases is very limited in Belgium, there is a clear willingness to insert whistle-blowing mechanisms in companies in order to reach an appropriate balance between, on the one hand, the risk of late alerts and their influence on the working atmosphere and, on the other hand, the need for transparency within companies. In addition, since it can involve the processing of personal data, whistle-blowing is subject to the provisions of the GDPR and of the Act of 30 July 2018 on the protection of privacy in relation to the processing of personal data. In this regard, the former Privacy Commission, now replaced by the Data Protection Authority, adopted a recommendation related to the compatibility of the whistle-blowing systems with the data protection legislation (Recommendation No. 1/2006 of 29 November 2006). The checklist of dos and don'ts in section 16.2 hereunder is based, among other things, on the said Recommendation.

Further, the EU has approved the Whistle Blowing Protection Directive 2019/1937 on 23 October 2019. This EU Directive should have been transposed by 17 December 2021, but Belgium, just like many other EU Member States, has missed the deadline. Below we set out the draft rules of the upcoming Belgian Whistle-Blower legislation, which will transpose the Directive. The material scope of the protection offered by the future legislation is only applicable to persons reporting breaches with regards to:

- public procurement;
- financial services, products and markets, and prevention of money laundering and terrorist financing;
- product safety and compliance;
- transport safety;
- protection of the environment;
- radiation protection and nuclear safety;
- food and feed safety, animal health and welfare;
- public health;
- consumer protection;
- protection of privacy and personal data, and security of network and information systems; and
- social fraud.

Belgium goes beyond the provision of the Directive by extending the scope to social fraud, which includes all breaches of the Social Penal Code. Almost all important employment and social security rules are enforced by the Social Penal Code. This means that the whistle-blowers will be protected when they report on breaches of employment law. The system is applicable to companies of fifty or more employees and provides protection to a wide scope of persons working in the private or public sector, who have acquired information on breaches, irrespective of whether they are, factually, employees, self-employed, freelance or civil servants.

The upcoming law demands the introduction of an internal reporting procedure to deal with whistle-blowing in order to prevent direct leaks to the public or press. In this way, companies would be obliged to confirm the receipt of a complaint within seven days and will have to give feedback to the reporter within three months. Also, external reporting processes to the authorities have to be made clear and easily accessible (by the Member States), and finally reporting publicly (to, e.g., the media or online) is addressed as a possibility when the reporters have reasonable grounds to believe that there is an imminent or manifest danger to the public interest or risk of irreversible damage.

Most interestingly, the Directive offers protection for whistle-blowers against any form of retaliation, including dismissal, negative evaluation, suspension, demotion, discrimination, etc. The violation of the whistle-blower rules will, i.a. be sanctioned by administrative fines and can lead to a lump sum compensation of up to twenty-eight weeks for reporting employees. This protection is awarded to reporters even if they reported anonymously (and were later identified) or if they had reasonable grounds to believe that the information was true at the time of the reporting (even when it turned out to be incorrect). Companies and authorities also have a duty of confidentiality relating to the identity of the reporters.

The Belgian draft legislation is assumed to be approved by Parliament before the Summer recess of 2022. However, for companies with 50 to 249 employees, the rules will only apply from 17 December 2023 onwards.

16.2. CHECKLIST OF DOS AND DON'TS

- Implement a whistle-blowing policy and ensure that the employees are duly informed. While awaiting the Belgian rules, companies of over fifty employees can already ensure the compatibility of their system with the rules of the EU Whistle-Blowing Directive and the provisions of the legislative proposal.
- Companies of over 250 employees should install an internal reporting channel.
- The scope and the purpose of the whistle-blowing system, as well as the admission procedure and report-handling process, must be described with precision (what can be reported by the whistle-blower, who can report or be reported, who is the person in charge of the processing, etc.).
- The report must be collected and processed by a person specifically appointed to hear complaints within the organization (this person must be bound to professional confidentiality, protected from pressure, work with autonomy and discretion, etc.).
- The whistle-blowing system is optional; it cannot impose reporting obligations on staff.
- Protection must be provided for the whistle-blower (against dismissal, discrimination, and harassment) and for the person against whom allegations have been made. The latter must be informed immediately and has the right to access, rectify, or delete the personal data concerning him/her.
- Subcontracting this investigative function in order to ensure independence and impartiality is possible if the provider respects the conditions normally applicable to the company (and the company will remain responsible).
- Whistle-blowing systems must observe the legal requirements of fairness, legality, and purpose (data protection legislation).

17. PROHIBITION OF DISCRIMINATION IN THE WORKPLACE

17.1. OVERVIEW OF ANTI-DISCRIMINATION LAWS

17.1.1. Legal Sources

The Belgian Constitution guarantees the equality of Belgian citizens and the equality between men and women (Article 10). It also guarantees the exercise of the rights and freedoms for all Belgian citizens without any discrimination. This also covers the rights and freedoms of the ideological and philosophical minorities (Article 11).

The framework of anti-discrimination legislation is mainly composed of three Acts:

(1) A general anti-discrimination Act of 10 May 2007 ('the General Act').
(2) An Act of 10 May 2007 on discrimination between men and women ('the Gender Act').
(3) An Act of 30 July 1981 aimed at the punishment of acts characterized by racist or xenophobic motives ('the Racism Act').

The anti-discrimination legislation is not applicable in cases qualified as harassment in the workplace. In such situations, the legislation on well-being at work is applicable (*see* section 13). Therefore, in a case where the discrimination also constitutes harassment, the victim may choose the grounds on which he/she wants to introduce the procedure. If it is based on the legislation on well-being at work, the anti-discrimination legislation will not apply. That said, the two legislations (on discrimination and on well-being) include the same types of protection mechanisms.

17.1.2. Common Principles

The following principles are identical in the three anti-discrimination acts:

– A prohibition on every form of *discrimination*, direct or indirect, on the basis of a number of grounds or criteria, called 'protected criteria'. Depending on the level of sensitiveness of the criterion, it will be less or more difficult to justify a *distinction* on the basis of the concerned criterion. Indirect discrimination occurs when a seemingly neutral term or criterion appears to be especially disadvantageous to certain people characterized by a given protected criterion in comparison to other people.
– There is a difference between the concept of 'discrimination', which is always illegal, and the concept of 'distinction', which can be justified and

permitted if there is a legitimate ground for the justification (*see* section 17.1.3). A distinction, which is not justified by a legitimate ground of justification, constitutes discrimination and is therefore prohibited.

– Compensation for damages in case of discrimination is either a lump sum amount equal to three to six times a monthly wage, depending on the circumstances, or the actual amount of the damage suffered (*see* section 17.1.4). The different acts also include penal sanctions.

– Protection against dismissal and any other detrimental measure related to the filing of a motivated complaint about discrimination. This protection also includes compensation for damages equal to a lump sum amount of six times a monthly wage or compensation for the actual damages suffered (*see* section 17.12).

The protected criteria are the following:

(1) General Act:
   (a) Sensitive criteria: age, sexual orientation, religious and philosophical conviction and handicap.
   (b) General Criteria: marital status, birth, wealth, political conviction, syndical conviction, language, current or future health condition, physical or genetic characteristics and social background.
(2) Gender Act: sex, including pregnancy, giving birth, maternity, paternity, co-motherhood, breastfeeding, sex change and gender identity, gender expression, gender characteristics, adoption and medically assisted reproduction.
(3) Racism Act: nationality, a so-called race, colour of skin, social background and national or ethnic origin.

Besides the explicitly protected criteria, a victim of discrimination can also revert to the common law liability rules. In this hypothesis, a victim must prove the existence of the three constitutive elements of this liability: (i) a fault; (ii) damage; and (iii) a causal link between fault and damage. The victim cannot benefit from compensation provided in the anti-discrimination legislation at the same time.

17.1.3. Distinction or Discrimination?

A *distinction*, which is based on a legitimate ground of justification, is *not discrimination*.

There are more or less strict *grounds of justification*, which can be summarized as follows:

(1) Direct distinction:

(a) *General criteria* in the General Act: (i) legitimate purpose; and (ii) the means to reach this purpose are appropriate and necessary.

(b) *Sensitive criteria* in the General Act and *criteria* in the Gender Act and Racism Act: the criterion must be an essential and defining requirement for the job.

(2) Indirect distinction:

(a) *All criteria, except handicap*: (i) legitimate purpose; and (ii) the means to reach this goal are appropriate and necessary.

(b) *Handicap*: proof that no reasonable modifications can be implemented.

A distinction, which should be regarded as discrimination, pursuant to the conditions set out above, could nevertheless be regarded as lawful if it is justified by one of the motives below:

(1) *General grounds* (for direct or indirect distinction, regarding all the criteria, except age and religious or philosophical conviction):

(a) *Measures of affirmative (or positive) action*, provided that certain conditions are met (for an extensive overview of the rules in this respect, *see* section 24).

(b) *A distinction dictated by law* which is in conformity with the Constitution, the law of the EU and international law.

(2) *Specific Grounds* (for direct distinction):

(a) *Age*: (i) legitimate purpose of the policy in the field of employment, labour market or any other comparable legitimate purpose; and (ii) the means to achieve that purpose are appropriate and necessary.

(b) *Religious or philosophical conviction*: the nature of the activities or the context in which they are being performed constitute an essential, legitimate and justifiable professional requirement, given the nature of the organization (applicable for organizations founded on the basis of a religious or philosophical conviction).

17.1.4. Means of Protection

Any provisions which are inconsistent with the anti-discrimination acts or stipulate that a contracting party renounces any rights granted by these acts are null and void.

Victims of discrimination and witnesses who testified are protected against detrimental measures taken by the employer (*see* section 17.12).

The employee (victim of discrimination) has a choice between compensation on a lump sum basis and compensation of the actual damage suffered. In the latter case, the employee has to prove the amount of the damage suffered.

The compensation on a flat rate basis is the following:

- six months of gross wages in all cases, except in the situations described below;
- three months of gross wages if it is proven that the disputed disadvantageous treatment would also have been carried through on non-discriminatory grounds;
- EUR 650.00 if the material damage can be redressed by application of the general nullity sanction;
- EUR 1,300.00 if the material damage can be redressed by application of the general nullity sanction, but: (i) there is no proof that the disputed disadvantageous treatment would also have been carried through on non-discriminatory grounds; or (ii) other circumstances justify a higher sum, such as the particular gravity of the moral damage suffered.

When a person presents facts before a court, which could lead to the suspicion of discrimination, it is up to the accused to prove that there is no discrimination.

17.1.5.   Cessation

Other than the above-mentioned compensations for damages, victims of discrimination can request the order of cessation of the discriminatory actions in the frame of a summary proceeding before the Labour Court.

This action for an injunction may be accompanied by measures, which are aimed at ensuring the execution of the decision:

- the payment of a periodic penalty payment; and
- displaying the judgment, at the expenses of the perpetrator, within or outside the buildings of the perpetrator and possible distribution in the media.

In case of a parallel criminal procedure, the action for an injunction to stop the discriminatory acts will be dealt with first.

17.2.   AGE DISCRIMINATION

Age discrimination is prohibited by the General Act.

However, a direct distinction based on age could be justified in two circumstances (*see also* section 17.1.3):

(1) if the age criterion is an essential and defining requirement for the job; or

(2) if the distinction is objectively and reasonably justified by an objective goal.

17.3. RACE DISCRIMINATION

Discrimination based on race is forbidden by the Racism Act.

As a distinction based on race will never serve a legitimate purpose, such distinctions cannot be justified on the basis of the general grounds of justification (*see* section 17.1.4).

17.4. SEX DISCRIMINATION/SEXUAL HARASSMENT

Sex discrimination is prohibited by the Gender Act.

However, sex distinction can be justified in certain circumstances (*see also* section 17.1.3):

(1) In case of direct distinction, if the sex criterion is an essential and defining requirement for the job.

(2) In case of indirect distinction, if this distinction serves a legitimate goal and if the means to reach this goal are appropriate and necessary.

(3) For both direct and indirect distinction, on the basis of the general grounds of justification, i.e.,:
    (a) measures of affirmative action; or
    (b) a distinction dictated by law.

With regard to the principle of equal pay between male and female employees, Belgium adopted an Act on reducing the gender pay gap on 22 April 2012. According to this Act, differences in pay and labour costs between men and women should be outlined in the company's annual audit ('social balance'). These annual audits are transmitted to the National Bank in order for them to be publicly available. Moreover, the Act stipulates that every two years, companies with over fifty employees should establish a comparative analysis of the wage structure of female and male employees. If this analysis shows that women earn less than men, the company will be required to produce an action plan. Finally, if discrimination is suspected, women can turn to their company's mediator, who will establish whether there is indeed a pay differential and, if so, they will try to find a compromise with the employer (*see* section 10.1.1).

In case of sexual harassment, the legislation on well-being at work will apply and not the anti-discrimination legislation. Both legislations guarantee the same level of protection (*see* sections 17.1.1 and 13.7).

17.5. HANDICAP AND DISABILITY DISCRIMINATION

The anti-discrimination Act of 10 May 2007 does not stipulate a definition for the terms 'disability' or 'handicap'. According to European jurisprudence, these concepts must be understood as referring to a limitation that results in a particular form of physical, mental or psychological impairments and which hinders the individual's professional life. It must also be probable that the limitation will last for a long time. Thus, it encompasses:

- physical and sensory health problems;
- chronic and degenerative diseases;
- genetic diseases;
- mental or intellectual limitations; and
- physical or mental restrictions as a result of a work accident or an occupational illness.

The General Act prohibits discrimination on the basis of a handicap or a current or future health condition. The refusal to provide reasonable accommodations for a disabled person constitutes discrimination. The government is planning to change the discrimination ground to 'health situation' in order to include the medical past, current and future health situation.

Currently, an employee's *medical past* is protected by CBA No. 95 of 10 October 2008 (CBA No. 95) concerning equal treatment during all phases of the labour relationship. This CBA is only applicable to private companies and not to the public sector. Besides an employee's medical past, CBA No. 95 also protects the following criteria: age, sex, sexual orientation, marital status, race, colour of skin, social background, national or ethnic origin, political or philosophical conviction, handicap and membership of a Union or other organization, if these criteria do not relate to the function or to the nature of the company, except where they are legally prescribed or permitted. This CBA does not include lump sum compensation with the intention of restoring the damage that is a consequence of the violation.

A direct or indirect distinction based on the *health condition* is only permitted if: (i) it is justified by a legitimate purpose; and (ii) the means to reach this purpose are appropriate and necessary (*see* section 17.1.3).

Direct distinction based on *handicap* is only permitted if this criterion constitutes an essential and defining requirement for the job. Indirect distinction based on handicap can only be justified if it is proven that no reasonable modifications to the working conditions can be implemented (*see* section 17.1.3). Reasonable modifications also extend to offering another vacant job within the company to the disabled employee.

For both *health condition* and *handicap*, the general grounds of justification, i.e., measures of affirmative action and distinction dictated by law, also apply.

17.6. NATIONAL ORIGIN DISCRIMINATION

Discrimination based on nationality is prohibited by the Racism Act.

However, foreign employees need to comply with regulations on work permits in order to be permitted to work in Belgium (*see* section 14).

Furthermore, a distinction based on nationality can be justified by one of the general grounds of justification (*see* section 17.1.3).

17.7. RELIGIOUS DISCRIMINATION

Discrimination based on religion and philosophical conviction is forbidden by the General Act.

However, a distinction based on these criteria can be justified if the nature of the activities or the context in which they are being performed constitutes an essential, legitimate and justifiable professional requirement, given the nature of the organization (applicable for organizations founded on the basis of a religious or philosophical conviction; *see* section 17.1.3).

17.8. MILITARY STATUS DISCRIMINATION

Military status is not protected as such in Belgian anti-discrimination legislation.

17.9. PREGNANCY DISCRIMINATION

Under Belgian law, pregnancy discrimination is a part of sex discrimination and is therefore prohibited by the Gender Act.

Maternity is also protected by the Labour Act of 16 March 1971. As of the moment that the employer is informed of the pregnancy, it cannot terminate the employment contract of the pregnant employee until one month after the postnatal leave has expired, except for reasons which are not related to the physical condition as a result of the pregnancy or delivery. This is without prejudice to the obligation of the employer to adapt to the working conditions of a pregnant employee if it is necessary to avoid exposing the employee to certain risks.

A distinction based on the pregnancy can be justified on the basis of the general grounds of justification, i.e., if this constitutes an essential and defining requirement for the job (direct distinction) or in case of a legitimate purpose and appropriate and necessary means (indirect distinction: *see* section 17.1.3). Theoretically, the other grounds of justification could also apply, i.e., measures of affirmative action or distinction dictated by law.

17.10.   MARITAL STATUS DISCRIMINATION

The General Act protects marital status.

A distinction based on marital status can nevertheless be justified on the basis of the general grounds of justification (*see* section 17.1.3).

17.11.   SEXUAL ORIENTATION DISCRIMINATION

The General Act prohibits sexual orientation discrimination.

A distinction based on sexual orientation can only be justified on the basis of the grounds applying to sensitive criteria, i.e., on the basis of an essential and defining requirement for the job (direct distinction), a legitimate purpose and appropriate and necessary means to attain this purpose (indirect distinction), measures of affirmative action or a distinction dictated by law (*see* section 17.1.3).

17.12.   RETALIATION

When an employee files a complaint on the basis of the anti-discrimination legislation, the employer cannot take 'detrimental measures' against the employee, except for reasons unrelated to the complaint.

Detrimental measures include, notably, the termination of the employment contract, the unilateral modification of working conditions and any prejudicial measure after the end of the employment contract (e.g., the non-issuance of social documents).

For the employee to be protected, the complaint must fulfil certain conditions ('motivated complaint'); i.e., it must: (i) be introduced at the company level in accordance with the internal policies of the company; (ii) be signed, dated and sent by registered letter; and (iii) explain the grievances vis-à-vis the perpetrator of the alleged discrimination. The protection also runs in case of legal action before a court.

The protection applies for the period of twelve months following the filing of the complaint or three months following the final judicial decision in case of judicial proceedings. During this period, if the employer takes a detrimental measure, it must prove that the measure is not linked to the complaint.

The employee affected by such detrimental measures has the possibility to ask the employer for his/her reintegration into the company under the same conditions as the ones applicable before the detrimental measures were taken. Alternatively, he/she can claim compensation for damages, consisting of a lump sum amount of six months of gross wages or compensation based on the actual damage suffered. This is without prejudice to the damages the employee can claim for the discrimination itself (*see* section 17.1.4).

The same kind of protection (no detrimental measures, a lump sum of six months of damages, etc.) applies to witnesses who testify during an internal company procedure or in court.

17.13. CONSTRUCTIVE DISMISSAL

Under Belgian law, an employee may invoke a 'constructive dismissal' when the employer unilaterally and substantially modifies an essential element of the employment contract. Generally, the employee will give notice to the employer to reinstate him/her under the conditions that were applicable before he/she invoked a 'constructive dismissal'. If the employer does not follow up on this formal notice, the employee can invoke a breach of contract by the employer and consequently claim an indemnity in lieu of notice.

Constructive dismissal is not often utilized in case of discrimination because, in this hypothesis, the employee loses his/her job, and if he/she erroneously invokes a constructive dismissal, he/she will have to pay an indemnity in lieu of notice to the employer. This risk can be avoided by initiating a procedure in judicial rescission, requesting the termination of the contract based on the wrongful conduct/measures of the employer, who will then have to pay damages generally equal to an indemnity in lieu of notice.

Usually, an employee who is a victim of discrimination will file an internal complaint about discrimination, as in this case he/she will keep his/her job, will be protected against dismissal and will have the possibility to seek damages if the discrimination is proven.

17.14.   CHECKLIST OF DOS AND DON'TS

– In order to reduce the risk of discrimination in the workplace, the most adequate tool is a *clear diversity policy,* which includes the principles applicable within the company, an indication of what is or is not allowed, and the internal procedures to be complied with if an employee wants to file a complaint about discrimination.
– The employees must also be sensitized to diversity and the risk of discrimination. In this view, the Belgian Interfederal Centre for Equal Opportunities 'Unia' provides 'best practices' that can be consulted online (www.unia.be).
– Finally, when a decision is made to terminate an employment contract or to modify working conditions, be sure that the reasons to do so are not discriminatory and keep evidence of these reasons.

18.   SMOKING IN THE WORKPLACE

18.1.   OVERVIEW

Over the past decades, social norms have shifted away from a widespread acceptance of tobacco smoking in everyday life to a general awareness of the health hazards of exposure to second-hand smoke, and hence the right to a smoke-free environment for all. While smoking employees were previously only required to show some 'courtesy' towards non-smokers, the Act of 22 December 2009 on smoke-free public spaces and the protection of employees against tobacco smoke ('the Act of 2009') now imposes a general ban on smoking in the workplace.

Every employer is required to guarantee a smoke-free environment for its employees, covering not only the actual workplace (offices, meeting rooms, hangars, etc.) but also other places that employees have access to in the course of their employment, such as lavatories, stairways, halls, restaurants, lifts, and relaxation rooms. The prohibition on smoking also applies to vehicles provided by an employer for the common transportation of employees. Even employees who have a separate office must abide by the non-smoking rule.

The Act of 2009 applies to all employers and employees, with the exception of: (1) closed drinking premises (e.g., a closed smoking room in a café) and casinos;[23] (2) private premises within psychiatric, geriatric or

---

23. A specific set of rules applies to the Hotel, Restaurant and Cafés (HORECA) industry. However, the prohibition would apply to the offices, hangars, depots, etc., where only employees have access. Hotel rooms are considered private spaces and would not fall within the scope of the prohibition.

general health or youth care institutions and prisons;[24] and (3) private homes. The ban on smoking would not apply to homeworkers and nurses who provide care to people in their private homes. However, if employees were employed in a separate workplace within one's house and home (e.g., a doctor's practice or a law office), the owner of the house would be considered an employer and would therefore have to abide by the non-smoking rule.

The employer must also take all necessary measures to inform all third parties who enter the company's premises (clients, delivery persons or other service providers) of the company's smoke-free environment in order to convince them to respect the ban on smoking.

As an exception to the rule, the employees, their Union representatives or the Health and Safety Committee may advise the employer of the possibility to install a smoking room within the company. However, this is a mere possibility and cannot be considered a smoker's right to counterbalance the non-smoker's right to a smoke-free environment. Specific technical regulations apply to certain aspects of smoking rooms (e.g., the ventilation system). Furthermore, the Health and Safety Committee must determine the time and duration of access to the smoking room in order to ensure non-smokers are not discriminated against as regards the working hours to be performed by all employees.

The law not only prohibits smoking, but it also prohibits anything that may incite people to smoke or lead them to believe smoking is authorized. Electronic cigarettes would thus fall under the scope of the smoking ban because of the fumes they exhume. Even if its fumes do not contain any tobacco, the electronic cigarette is created to look like a normal cigarette. It could therefore be considered as encouraging smoking and hence is inadmissible in the workplace.

The non-compliance with the prohibition to smoke at the workplace is sanctioned by Article 133 of the Social Penal Code with a penal fine of up to EUR 8,000 or an administrative fine of up to EUR 4,000. In case the non-compliance has caused health damage to a worker, the article prescribes a prison sentence of six months to three years, a penal fine of up to EUR 48,000 or an administrative fine of up to EUR 24,000. However, only the employer and his appointee or trustee can be held responsible, not the smoking employee.

---

24. The public services in charge of these institutions are to establish the rules applicable to the use of tobacco within their premises, applicable to the inhabitants and their visitors.

18.2.   CHECKLIST OF DOS AND DON'TS

- Post non-smoking signs at the reception and other areas of the workplace (restaurants, lavatories, depots, etc.).
- Ban smoking in the workplace, except in designated areas outside.
- Alternatively, if so advised by the Health and Safety Committee, install a smoking room inside, compliant with all technical and health and safety regulations.
- Draft a Smoking Policy as part of the Work Rules, defining conditions of smoking breaks (time, duration, impact on working hours).

19.   USE OF DRUGS AND ALCOHOL IN THE WORKPLACE

19.1.   OVERVIEW

The negative impact of drug and alcohol abuse on the individual employee and the company can hardly be overstated. Certain studies have shown that an employee with serious alcohol dependency will lose up to 25% of his/her normal productivity.[25] Moreover, alcohol and drug abuse has both physical and psychological effects on the employee and his environment and gives rise to high health care costs.

Workplace drug testing is a complex topic. Drug and alcohol use is considered related to the health situation of an employee and therefore are sensitive, private data. Many rules protect the individual's right to privacy and prohibit the processing of personal data related to health.

At the international level, Article 12 of the Universal Declaration of Human Rights explicitly states that no one shall be subjected to arbitrary interference with his/her privacy. Also, in its 1996 Code of Practice on Management of alcohol and drug-related issues in the workplace, the International Labour Organization stated that testing should be undertaken in accordance with national laws and practices. At the European level, the European Convention on Human Rights (ECHR) also guarantees the right to privacy, except in the interest of national security, public safety or the economic well-being of the country, for the prevention of disorder and crime, for the protection of health and morals, or for the protection of the rights and freedoms of others (Article 8).

However, an employee's right to privacy ends where his/her and his/her co-worker's health and safety in the workplace are at stake. Under Article 13(2)(d) of European Directive 89/391/EEC on the introduction of measures to encourage improvements in the safety and health of employees, the employee must immediately inform the employer and/or the employees with

---

25. Numbers published by the National Office of Public Health.

specific responsibility for the safety and health of employees in any work situation, that he/she has reasonable grounds for considering to represent a serious and immediate danger to health and safety.

At the national level, Article 22 of the Constitution guarantees the individual's right to the protection of his/her privacy. This right is not absolute and may therefore be restricted, provided: (1) the intrusion on a person's privacy serves a legitimate goal; (2) the limitation of the right is proportionate to the achievement of this goal;[26] and (3) the restriction has a legal basis, i.e., is founded on precise rules. The 1996 Act on the well-being of employees (the 'Well-Being Act') is a legitimate restriction on the right to privacy, in that it imposes the obligation on every employer to take all necessary measures to ensure the well-being of its employees in the course of their employment by applying the general principles on the prevention of risks.

Specifically, with regard to the prevention of alcohol and drugs, the Social Partners entered into CBA No. 100 with a view towards obliging employers to set up an efficient drug and alcohol prevention policy and setting out the minimum requirements that such a policy should meet.

This goal is to be reached in two stages: a compulsory one and an optional one. First and foremost, every employer must draft a 'declaration of intent' setting out the general intention of its policy on alcohol and drug prevention. This 'declaration of intent' had to be inserted within the Work Rules since 1 April 2010. This is the compulsory stage.

In the second stage, the employer can but is not obliged to further implement this policy by outlining specific procedures and measures to achieve this goal. These measures may vary depending on the size of the company, the nature of its activities and the workforce.

CBA No. 100 outlines a framework of four minimum requirements any efficient policy should meet, i.e.,: (i) prevention and education; (ii) specific rules applicable to all staff; (iii) procedures on how to deal with problematic behaviour; and (iv) help and assistance to be provided by professional caretakers. CBA No. 100 sets out a general framework but ultimately leaves it up to the employers to define their individual policies. The flexibility which CBA No. 100 offers to employers is, at the same time, its weakness: employers may find themselves at a loss as to how to actually implement the vague and general principles set out by the CBA.

If an employer wishes to submit employees to alcohol and drug tests prior to entrusting them with specific tasks, it may only do so under strict conditions to be laid down within the Work Rules. These rules must determine the nature of the tests, the (groups of) employees that may be

---

26. If less invasive solutions are available, these should be preferred. The invasion of a person's privacy is thus allowed as a 'last resort', i.e., if the legitimate goal cannot be achieved by other means.

submitted to these tests, the procedure to be followed, persons who are qualified to submit employees to the test, the time of testing and possible consequences of a positive test.

Moreover, the tests may only be used with a view toward preventing risks at work and not for any other purpose (e.g., sanctioning the employee), they must be adequate and not excessive, the employee must agree to be tested, and the results must not be processed in a database, given their sensitive nature. At all times, the proceedings as set out by the employer should meet with the general principles of finality, proportionality and legitimacy as set out above.

In the course of the recruitment process, enquiries as to a person's legal or illegal use of drugs can only be made for reasons that are related to the current ability of the applicant and the specific requirements of the job. To that effect, only the Prevention Advisor-Occupational Physician is allowed to ask these questions and submit the applicants to biological or medical tests and the gathering of verbal information on the applicant's health or family history (Act of 28 January 2003 on medical examinations within the framework of labour relations). With the applicant's prior consent, this occupational physician will have to conduct his/her various biological examinations (blood, breath, saliva, urine) within the strict legal framework aimed at assessing the applicant's health condition as a requirement for fulfilling a job that entails specific safety risks for him/herself and his/her colleagues (e.g., operators of cranes, motorized engines, or jobs that require the manipulation of food). These medical tests can only be carried out after a job offer has been made.

In view of the applicant's obligation to act in good faith during the recruitment process, he/she must provide the employer with all information that might be relevant to the employer and the nature of his/her function. If the applicant refuses to submit him/herself to the tests that are deemed necessary and justified by the occupational physician, he/she cannot be recruited.

Only occupational physicians are allowed to carry out the biological tests. In view of the employer's obligation to ensure the safety of its employees in the workplace, it would be permitted to conduct non-biological tests (e.g., asking him/her to walk a straight line) when confronted with an employee who shows signs of intoxication and who may pose a safety risk.

19.2. CHECKLIST OF DOS AND DON'TS

- Insert a 'declaration of intent' within the Work Rules, setting out the general purpose of a policy on the prevention of alcohol and drug use within the company (mandatory).

- Raise awareness and provide training to leading staff on how to deal with alcohol and drug-related issues (recommended).
- Create a framework for Prevention Advisors competent for occupational health or psychosocial risks, as well as for social workers to provide assistance and help for dysfunctional employees.
- Rely on professionals (e.g., the Prevention Advisor-Occupational Physician) if an applicant for a job involving safety risks is to be submitted to further tests upon having completed the application process.

20. AIDS, HIV, SARS, BLOOD-BORNE PATHOGENS

20.1. OVERVIEW

Belgian law prohibits any discrimination, directly or indirectly, based upon the current or future health situation of an applicant or employee. This prohibition applies from the start of the recruitment process, throughout the employee's employment and up to the end of the employment contract.

Medical testing[27] prior to hiring the employee may only take place within the strict framework of the Act of 28 January 2003 by the Prevention Advisor-Occupational Physician in order to assess the applicant's current aptitude for a job that entails specific safety requirements. Testing for AIDS or predictive genetic examinations are strictly prohibited under Article 3, § 2 of this Act. The Act contains no specific prohibition with regard to other blood-borne pathogens[28] or diseases such as SARS.[29]

However, as with other ailments or illnesses, an employer is only permitted to enquire as to the employee's or applicant's current state of health if this information is relevant because of the nature of the job and the conditions for carrying it out. Only after a job offer has been made could the applicant be submitted to tests by the Prevention Advisor-Occupational Physician, if the job implies a safety post or vigilance post, or for work that entails the handling of or contact with food substances or if the applicant would be asked to drive motorized engines, cranes or hoists when this driving could endanger the security and safety of other employees.

During his/her recruitment process, the applicant should, in good faith, communicate his/her condition to his/her future employer, who will have to inform him/her of possible negative effects the job might have on his/her

---

27. These medical tests can be a general physical examination, as well as x-rays, bone scans, or hearing and vision tests.
28. Blood-borne pathogens are germs that live in human blood and can cause diseases such as Hepatitis B or C, causing infections and liver damage.
29. A possibly fatal respiratory disease caused by a virus – the last outbreak dates back to 2002–2003.

existing ailment. Failure to do so may lead to the employer's liability for additional health care costs, should the employee's condition worsen.

20.2.   CHECKLIST OF DOS AND DON'TS

– Treat all applicants on an equal basis during the application process.
– Do not ask questions about an applicant's personal health or personal life unless this information pertains to specific job requirements and is related to the applicant's current ability to perform the job.
– Never submit candidates to tests for HIV-AIDS and predictive genetic research.
– Inform applicants of the impact the job might have on potential medical conditions of the applicant.

21.   DRESS AND GROOMING REQUIREMENTS

21.1.   OVERVIEW

Where it is necessary, an employer has to provide specific work attire aimed at preventing clothes from becoming soiled. This matter is regulated by the Royal Decree of 6 July 2004 regarding work attire. Beyond that, there are no specific rules and regulations on how to dress in the workplace. An employer is allowed to impose a dress code on its employees if it can prove that such a dress code is based on reasonable grounds. This would be the case if: (1) the dress code is aimed at achieving a legitimate goal; (2) its requirements are proportionate to achieving this goal; and (3) they are firmly embedded in a policy, known and applicable to all employees.

The right to dress in a way one sees fit can also be considered an element of an employee's personal privacy. Especially when the personal dress is felt to be an expression of one's personal belief or religion (e.g., a headscarf), a conflict may arise between an employer's dress code and the employee's right not to be discriminated against on the grounds of personal belief or religion.

In general, the Labour Courts tend to allow employers to adhere to the principle of neutrality and hence to prohibit all sorts of religious dress in the workplace. In a decision of 9 March 2015, the Supreme Court (*Hof van Cassatie – Cour de cassation*) requested a preliminary ruling from the ECJ on the question of whether Article 2.2 a) of European Directive 2000/78/EC should be interpreted as implying that the prohibition for a Muslim to wear a headscarf in the workplace does not amount to direct discrimination if the rule prohibits all employees from wearing signs adhering to any philosophy, religion or politics in the workplace.

In the 'Achbita' judgment of 14 March 2017,[30] the ECJ ruled that Article 2.2 a) of European Directive 2000/78/EC must be interpreted as meaning that the prohibition on wearing an Islamic headscarf, which arises from an internal rule of a private undertaking prohibiting the visible wearing of any political, philosophical or religious sign in the workplace, does not constitute direct discrimination based on religion or belief within the meaning of that Directive.

By contrast, such an internal rule of a private undertaking may constitute indirect discrimination within the meaning of Article 2.2 b) of European Directive 2000/78 if it is established that the apparently neutral obligation it imposes results, in fact, in persons adhering to a particular religion or belief being put at a particular disadvantage, unless it is objectively justified by a legitimate aim, such as the pursuit by the employer, in its relations with its customers, of a policy of political, philosophical and religious neutrality, and the means of achieving that aim are appropriate and necessary.

The Supreme Court and the Labour Court of Appeal of Ghent have (more or less) followed the judgment of the CJEU and ruled that there was no discrimination in the case.[31]

In 2021, the ECJ has nuanced its Achbita case law in the joint cases WABE and Müller Handels by stating that a neutrality principle should be based on a genuine need of the employer.[32] Such a genuine need can be demonstrated, in the first place, by the rights and legitimate wishes of customers or users. That is the case, for example, of parents' right to ensure the education and teaching of their children in accordance with their religious, philosophical and teaching beliefs. However, this cannot be justified by discriminatory requirements on the part of customers. In the second place, an employer could argue that, in the absence of a neutrality policy, its freedom to conduct a business, would be undermined in that, given the nature of its activities or the context in which they are carried out, it would suffer adverse consequences. For example, both the prevention of social conflicts and the presentation of a neutral image of the employer vis-à-vis customers may correspond to a real need on the part of the employer, which it is for the latter to demonstrate.

Failure to meet dress requirements can also lead to an employee's dismissal. This dismissal may be deemed abusive if the judge finds that the parties failed to make any specific arrangement on what to wear at work, and

---

30. ECJ, 14 Mar. 2017, *Samira Achbita, Centrum voor gelijkheid van kansen en voor racismebestrijding v. G4S Secure Solutions NV*, Case C-157/15.
31. Supreme Court, 9 Oct. 2017, No. S.12.0062.N; Labour Court of Appeal Ghent, 12 Oct. 2020. AR 2019/AG/55.
32. ECJ 15 Jul. 2021, *IX v WABE eV (C804/18), and MH Müller Handels GmbH v MJ*, C804/18 and C341/19.

among others, CBA No. 81 on electronic communication, CBA No. 68 on security cameras and CBA No. 100 on alcohol tests. In all of these cases, the information may be collected by the employer within certain limits and provided that it complies with an ad hoc procedure lying down the criteria set out in Article 8 ECHR (purpose, proportionality, and transparency of the control). For instance, CBA No. 81 on employees' privacy with regard to the monitoring of electronic communication network data determines for what purposes and under which conditions of proportionality and transparency such control can be installed, and in which manner the individualization of such data is permitted. The control may only cover *data* (i.e., electronic communications, data transiting through networks understood in the broad sense, including IP addresses, time and duration of websites visited, size of e-mails, etc.) which is to be distinguished from the *content* (text message of e-mails, pictures and documents sent, etc.) of the communication, and it may only occur for four purposes: (i) for the prevention of unlawful or defamatory facts; (ii) for the protection of economic, commercial and financial interests; (iii) for the security and/or good technical functioning of IT network systems of the company; and (iv) for compliance in good faith with the principles and rules of the use of technology. When installing the data control system, the employer must inform the employees concerned and their representatives (e.g., Works Council) on all aspects of the control.

22.1.1.   Transfer of Personal Data

The GDPR ensures the free movement of data within the EU (Article 1, § 3), while at the same time providing that any transfer of personal data which are undergoing processing or are intended for processing after transfer to a third country or to an international organization shall take place only if, subject to the other provisions of the GDPR, some conditions are complied with by the controller and processor, including for onward transfers of personal data from the third country or an international organization to another third country or to another international organization (Article 44).

22.1.2.   European Data Protection Legislation

On 4 May 2016, the GDPR was published in the Official Journal of the EU. It entered into force on 24 May 2016, and it has been applicable since 25 May 2018. The GDPR aims to uniformize and reinforce the existing various national data protection legislations. More specifically, Belgium adopted the Act of 3 December 2017, which partially implements the GDPR with the creation of a supervisory Data Protection Authority (Article 51 GDPR), replacing the former Privacy Commission. In addition, the Act of 30 July 2018 replaces the old privacy act of 1992 and, *inter alia*, provides the national implementation and specification of the GDPR rules.[35]

The GDPR provides for a single set of rules applicable to European and non-European companies offering online services in the EU. With the introduction of the 'one-stop-shop' principle, companies that operate in Europe now only have to deal with one single supervisory Data Protection Authority, which is represented in Belgium by the Belgian Data Protection Authority. The regulation also seeks to enhance the level of data protection for individuals whose personal data are processed and gives them more control over their data. First, the GDPR lays down six principles that need to be adhered to for legitimate processing of personal data:

(1) *Lawfulness, fairness and transparency.* The data should be processed lawfully, fairly and in a transparent manner in relation to the data subject.

(2) *Purpose Limitation.* The data should be collected for specified, explicit and legitimate purposes and not further processed in a manner that is incompatible with those purposes.

(3) *Data minimization.* The personal data should be adequate, relevant and limited to what is necessary in relation to the purposes for which they are processed.

(4) *Accuracy.* The personal data should be accurate and, where necessary, kept up-to-date. This also entails a right to correct or erase incorrect data.

(5) *Storage limitation.* The personal data shall be kept in a form that permits the identification of data subjects for no longer than is necessary for the purposes for which the personal data are processed.

(6) *Integrity and confidentiality.* The personal data shall be processed in a manner that ensures appropriate security of the personal data, including protection against unauthorized or unlawful processing and against accidental loss, destruction or damage, using appropriate technical or organizational measures.

Regarding the lawfulness of the processing, Article 6 of the GDPR provides for six legal grounds for the processing of personal data:

(a) the data subject has given consent to the processing of his or her personal data for one or more specific purposes;

(b) processing is necessary for the performance of a contract to which the data subject is a party or in order to take steps at the request of the data subject prior to entering into a contract;

---

35. The Act of 30 Jul. 2018 should be seen as the complementary or specific rules, while the GDPR contains the general rules which are in principle applicable.

(c) processing is necessary for compliance with a legal obligation to which the controller is subject;

(d) processing is necessary in order to protect the vital interests of the data subject or of another natural person;

(e) processing is necessary for the performance of a task carried out in the public interest or in the exercise of official authority vested in the controller;

(f) processing is necessary for the purposes of the legitimate interests pursued by the controller or by a third party, except where such interests are overridden by the interests or fundamental rights and freedoms of the data subject which require protection of personal data, in particular where the data subject is a child.

In general, employers will have to limit themselves to processing grounds b (data which is necessary for the performance of the employment contract, e.g., for the payment of the salary), c (the personal data which is necessary to comply with the legal rules, e.g., in relation to the obligation to draft social documents) and f (the legitimate interests of the employer, e.g., when screening applicants for a vacancy). The vital interest (ground d) and public interest (ground e) are not easily accepted by an employer. What concerns the consent of the data subject (ground a) is that there is an ongoing legal discussion as to whether an employee can freely give his 'free consent' to his employer. The majority holds the position that an employee cannot freely consent to the processing of data by his employer because of the hierarchical nature of the employment relationship, which makes it very difficult for the employee to refuse as the employee will feel pressured to accept the processing. The consent of an employee will only be accepted as a valid processing ground if there are neither possible negative consequences nor benefits for the employer.

In case sensitive categories of personal data are involved, such as data revealing racial or ethnic origin, political opinions, religious or philosophical beliefs, sexual orientation or Trade Union membership, as well as genetic, biometric or medical data, the GDPR has further limited the legal processing grounds. In this case, there is, e.g., no legal processing ground when it is necessary for the purpose of the legitimate interests of the employer. Data subjects have the right to withdraw consent at any time, as well as the right to be fully and unambiguously informed about what happens to personal data once they are processed. Moreover, employees have the right to have access to, rectify or erase personal data (*the right to be forgotten*) or to transmit them to a third party (*data portability*). The employer's obligation to process data as securely as possible is also reinforced; employers may, under certain circumstances, be required to seek recourse to privacy-enhancing techniques such as anonymization, pseudonymization and encryption, in order to comply with the GDPR's principles.

Employees can file a complaint with the Belgian Data Protection Authority, which has the legal authority to inspect the employer and levy sanctions upon the employer. With penalties rising up to EUR 20 million or 4% of a company's global turnover, compliance with the GDPR, as well as the ability to be able to demonstrate one's compliance, is paramount. The Conflict Resolution Chamber of the Data Protection Authority has become rather active during the last years and has already fined several employers (in some cases, a warning sufficed). Until now, the fines have varied from several EUR 1,000 up to more than EUR 100,000.

22.2. CHECKLIST OF DOS AND DON'TS

– Revise and adapt your IT and data protection policies in order to comply with the GDPR (and the specifications in the Act of 30 July 2018). A clear IT/data protection policy should define, e.g., how the Internet and e-mails can be used at work (private and/or professional), who has access to employees' personal data, who in the company is responsible for data protection, how an individual can have access to his/her data, how monitoring by the employer is conducted, how employees can give and withdraw their consent, what are the conditions for data portability and data transfer, etc.
– Make sure such a policy is in the correct language (Dutch, French or German, depending on the location of the operational unit of the company).
– Notify the Data Protection Authority if surveillance cameras are used.
– Maintain a record of processing activities under your responsibility containing all of the elements of information required by law.

23. WORKPLACE INVESTIGATIONS FOR COMPLAINTS OF DISCRIMINATION, HARASSMENT, FRAUD, THEFT AND WHISTLE-BLOWING

23.1. OVERVIEW

23.1.1. Discrimination and Harassment

In cases of discrimination or harassment, the employee may ask the employer to investigate the denounced facts and to take appropriate measures (*see* sections 17 and 13.7).

The employee may make an informal request for an investigation to the employer, to his/her superior or to an employee representative, or file a formal and *motivated complaint* for discrimination (to be addressed to the employer; *see* section 17.12) or a *formal demand for intervention* for harassment (to be addressed to the Prevention Advisor-Psychosocial Risks at Work; *see* section 13.7). This procedure must be specifically explained in the company's Work Rules.

Ideally, the internal procedure should result in the cessation of the discrimination or harassment, so that the employee does not have to revert to an external body.

However, if the situation does not improve, or if the internal procedure is not compliant (e.g., no decision in due time), the employee may file a complaint to the Inspectorate well-being at work (Ministry of Work), to the Public Prosecutor or to the Labour Court. The latter will then ensure, together with the employer, that the internal procedure meets the legal requirements.

The complaint to the Public Prosecutor is often used by the employee to obtain evidence. Indeed, the Public Prosecutor can decide to hear witnesses, and their testimony will be added to the criminal file. Even if the Public Prosecutor decides not to prosecute, the employee may obtain a copy of the criminal case record, and on this basis, claim damages before the Labour Court.

23.1.2. Fraud, Theft, Whistle-Blowing

There is no specific legislation in Belgium, which governs workplace investigations. Employers are, therefore, free to decide whether or not to implement specific measures to check on their employees (surveillance cameras, e-mail monitoring under certain conditions, body searches, etc.). Such procedures and measures must, of course, be compliant with the legal rules on employees' privacy (*see* section 22).

In particular, the Act of 10 April 1990 on private security and CBA No. 89 of 30 January 2007 on theft prevention and controls in the workplace establish a limited right for employers to carry out *entry* and *exit* inspections at the workplace. However, inspections on the work floor (inside the premises) are not regulated by law. Body searches and controls at the exit of the workplace can be carried out in order to prevent or discover theft, whereas controls at the entry of a workplace may only occur to prevent the entry of weapons or dangerous items in the workplace. Workplace inspections (e.g., body searches, personal locker controls and desk and drawer controls by the employer), although not regulated by law, are generally authorized if the employee gives his/her consent and is present during the control and if the principles of purpose, legality (procedures inserted within the Work Rules or internal policy) and proportionality are observed.

More and more importance is attached to whistle-blowing in Belgium. As indicated in section 16, the *whistle-blowing* procedure is a mechanism enabling individuals to report the conduct of a member of their organization that appears contrary to a law, regulation or basic rules established by the organization. An adequate definition of such a mechanism is essential to prevent unjustified alerts and to deal efficiently with legitimate ones. The importance of whistle-blowing mechanisms is certain to increase in the coming years, as Belgium is implementing the EU Whistle-Blowing Directive in 2022 (*see* section 16).

Within the exercise of their tasks, social inspectors have the right to enter business premises or places subject to their control day and night, without prior warning (Article 23 of the Social Penal Code), and may examine, control and collect any information they consider relevant to ensure the observance of the provisions they supervise. When they deem it necessary, social inspectors may request the assistance of the police.

23.2.   CHECKLIST OF DOS AND DON'TS

− Be sure to have compliant internal procedures for discrimination and harassment cases.
− If a complaint is filed by an external body (i.e., the Social Inspectorate well-being at work or the Public Prosecutor), immediately communicate the internal policies and the name of the persons involved in order to assure these external bodies that the facts will be internally investigated and that adequate measures will be taken.
− In case of harassment, always involve the Prevention Advisor-Psychosocial Risks at Work before adapting the working conditions of the plaintiff or the person against whom the complaint has been filed. Implement a simple, clear and effective whistle-blowing policy in your company in order to resolve grievances internally.
− Implement a Code of Conduct aimed at preventing criminal offences and fostering ethical practices.

24. AFFIRMATIVE ACTION/NON-DISCRIMINATION REQUIREMENTS

24.1. OVERVIEW

The anti-discrimination legislation states that a direct or indirect distinction based on a protected criterion (age, marital status, sexual orientation, etc.) cannot be considered as discrimination if this direct or indirect distinction is based on affirmative action (*see* section 17).

Affirmative action is subject to the following conditions:

– there must be a manifest inequality;
– the eradication of this inequality should be an appointed goal;
– the measure of affirmative action should be limited in time and should cease to exist once the goal is attained;
– the measure of affirmative action should not needlessly limit someone else's rights.

The Royal Decree of 11 February 2019 constitutes the framework for positive actions, setting forward the procedures and conditions on the basis of which an employer can take positive actions. It sets three years as the maximum duration of a positive action and provides the introduction procedure of a positive action plan, which necessitates a CBA or an accession plan. In case the employer opts for an accession plan, the employees will be able to give remarks, and any disputes with the employer will have to be resolved through mediation or by a decision of the sectoral Joint Commission. Therefore, it is not possible to simply unilaterally impose a positive action plan.

However, already before the adoption of the Royal Decree of 11 February 2019, several measures constituting affirmative actions were set out in Acts, regulations and some employers' recruitment campaigns in order to address specific discrimination towards women, disabled people, young employees and homosexuals.

Moreover, legislative initiatives in Belgium are intended to stimulate rather than impose. This approach is well exemplified by the facultative Code of Conduct which was agreed upon by the representative employers' and employees' organizations in 2008 and which seeks to promote certain good practices (e.g., a Code of Conduct at the company level, company diversity plans and measures of affirmative action).

However, there is a quota for the employment of people with disabilities in the public sector (which ranges between 2.5% and 3% depending on the governmental level).

Furthermore, a law was voted on in 2012 to reduce the salary gap between men and women. The main idea is to make the salary gap more visible and transparent in order to allow the Social Partners to negotiate and decrease the gap. In view of this, certain measures have been taken (e.g., the drafting of an analysis report on the remuneration structure at a company level and a gender test for the functions' classification at the industry level: *see* section 10.1.1).

24.2.   CHECKLIST OF DOS AND DON'TS

– Be aware that an employer cannot implement a positive action plan without the involvement of the employees or their representatives.
– Before taking any action related to employees, verify that some of them will not be affected in a more detrimental way than others.
– Implement clear internal policies in order to avoid discrimination and an internal complaint procedure if a discrimination case nonetheless arises.

25.   RESOLUTION OF LABOUR, DISCRIMINATION AND EMPLOYMENT DISPUTES: LITIGATION, ARBITRATION, MEDIATION AND CONCILIATION

25.1.   INTERNAL DISPUTE RESOLUTION PROCESS

In cases where an employee faces a disciplinary procedure, only the sanctions provided for in the Work Rules can be taken. Furthermore, the Work Rules must contain the possibilities of redress that are open to employees who have grievances or who wish to make observations on, or object to, sanctions imposed on them.

The Trade Union Delegation within the company has the right to be heard by the employer in relation to each actual or potential collective conflict. Moreover, every employee has the right to be assisted by a Trade Union Delegate if he/she has an individual grievance.

25.2.   MEDIATION AND CONCILIATION

25.2.1.   Collective Labour Law

If the employer and the Trade Union Delegation cannot settle a collective dispute, they may call upon the secretary of the Unions.

If there is still no solution, the matter can be referred to the so-called Conciliation Committee of the Joint Committee. This Conciliation Committee is comprised of the chairman of the Joint Committee (which is a civil servant) and members appointed on an equal basis between employers' organizations and Trade Unions.

Yet, conciliation before the Joint Committee will always be on a voluntary basis. Parties cannot be forced to settle their dispute. The purpose of the conciliation procedure is to bring the parties together to reach an agreement. The conciliator does not make a judgment nor suggest a solution but works with the parties to find an acceptable outcome.

Another option is to seek assistance from the Social Dialogue Department of the Federal Public Service for Employment, which has created an office of mediators to help resolve collective labour disputes. The mediator goes a step further and makes suggestions to the parties on a possible solution.

25.2.2.   Individual Labour Law

Conciliation is organized by the court. Either party can ask the court to start a conciliation procedure before any litigation procedure in court has started or at any time during the litigation procedure. A judge can also propose conciliation to the parties rather than a trial. It is then up to the parties to agree or not.

However, conciliation is rarely used.

Mediation is a procedure by which an impartial third party, the mediator, helps two or more people in a dispute attempt to reach an agreement.

There are two types of mediation, namely: (i) a voluntary mediation, which is not linked to existing legal proceedings; or (ii) a court-instigated mediation, which takes place within the framework of existing legal proceedings but only with the parties' consent.

The parties will jointly choose the mediator. Mediators are accredited by the Federal Public Service of Justice and are usually lawyers.

The success of mediation leads to a settlement agreement that is binding on the parties. However, unlike an arbitral award, this agreement is not enforceable, nor is it appealable. If enforcement of the agreement becomes necessary, the party needs to go to court to seek judicial ratification.

A mediation procedure has the advantage of avoiding confrontation, which is particularly useful when the employer and the employee have to maintain their working relationship. The procedure is more rapid than a 'normal' judicial proceeding before the court, which means that the problem could be settled in a short period of time.

25.3.   ARBITRATION

As a general rule, any dispute that can be resolved by a settlement agreement (and thus no dispute with regard to public order provisions) may be submitted to arbitration.

As a basic principle, the employer and the employee can only decide to resort to arbitration after the dispute has arisen. In other words, it is not possible to enter into an arbitration clause beforehand (e.g., within the employment contract), indicating that in case of conflict, the matter will be presented to an arbitrator instead of the Labour Court.

There is one exception to this rule: an arbitral clause may be inserted within the employment contract for employees earning at least EUR 73,571.00 gross per year (inclusive of benefits; the figure in 2021, yearly indexed) and entrusted with high management responsibilities (i.e., the daily management of the company or of a significant part of the company).

An arbitral award is final and binding on the parties, and it is not possible to appeal an arbitral award before a court.

The most important arbitration institute in Belgium is the CEPANI-CEPINA (Belgian Centre for National and International Arbitration), based in Brussels. However, in Belgium, few employment law cases are presented to arbitrators.

25.4.   LITIGATION

Belgium has a specialized jurisdiction for labour conflicts, namely the Labour Tribunals, sentencing in the first instance, and the Labour Courts of Appeal, sentencing at the appellate level.

Procedures before the Labour Courts are regulated by the Judicial Code, as is the case for all civil and commercial procedures in Belgium. There are only a few rules that are specific to the Labour Courts, namely:

- the possibility for a Trade Union representative to represent the employee in court;
- the unlimited possibility of appeal (a judgment of a Labour Tribunal can always be appealed, irrespective of the value of the claim); and
- the presence of a specific Public Prosecutor in certain social matters (the Labour Prosecutor).

Belgian employment litigation is based on a system of civil law. In principle, case law precedents have no legally binding force. Yet, in practice, decisions of the highest courts have strong persuasive authority, especially when confirmed repeatedly.

The Labour Courts have jurisdiction with regard to all individual labour disputes (e.g., termination of employment contracts, salary, equal treatment and unfair competition). In principle, they have no jurisdiction with regard to collective labour law conflicts. Yet, they can impose a sentence in some situations of a 'collective nature' where 'disputes of rights' are concerned. Finally, the Labour Courts are also competent for all claims related to social security issues, as well as for all social assistance matters.

25.5. FINES, PENALTIES AND DAMAGES

25.5.1. Social Penal Code

Infringements of employment laws are often sentenced to criminal sanctions included within the Social Penal Code.

The Social Penal Code distinguishes four levels of sanctions, depending on the gravity of the violation of the law:

(1) Level 1: administrative fine from EUR 10 to EUR 100.
(2) Level 2: criminal fine from EUR 50 to EUR 500 or administrative fine from EUR 25 to EUR 250.
(3) Level 3: criminal fine from EUR 100 to EUR 1,000 or administrative fine from EUR 50 to EUR 500.
(4) Level 4: imprisonment from six months to three years and criminal fine from EUR 600 to EUR 6,000 or administrative fine from EUR 300 to EUR 3,000.

All of these amounts are subject to a multiplication factor (currently 8), which substantially elevates the fines:

– Level 1: administrative fine from EUR 80 to EUR 800.
– Level 2: criminal fine from EUR 400 to EUR 4,000 or administrative fine from EUR 200 to EUR 2,000.
– Level 3: criminal fine from EUR 800 to EUR 8,000 or administrative fine from EUR 400 to EUR 4,000.
– Level 4: imprisonment from six months to three years and criminal fine from EUR 4,800 to EUR 48,000 or administrative fine from EUR 2,400 to EUR 24,000.

Moreover, for certain infringements, the number of employees concerned by the infringement multiplies the sanction.

Next to the fines and imprisonment, the Social Penal Code also foresees the possibility to impose an operating ban of one to three years, a professional ban of one to three years (prohibition to perform a profession which includes counselling employers or employees in their obligations relating to Social Law) or the closure of a company. In addition, the Criminal Court could also condemn the perpetrator to the payment of social security contribution, a community service or the forfeiture of illegal gains.

The most common infringements identified by the Social Inspection are those related to breaches of internal work rules regulations (especially working time), breaches of CBAs, social documents, wage protection and part-time work. However, infringements leading the most to an actual criminal prosecution are related to illegal or undeclared work, part-time employment, employment of foreign workers, forgery, social documents and obstructing of surveillance by the Social Inspection. Infringements of provisions that are prescribed with sanctions of levels 3 and 4 make up to 75% of the crimes brought before the Labour Prosecutor. Most levels 1 and 2 infringements are dealt with by the Social Inspection itself (e.g., by giving a warning or a deadline to comply with the law).

25.5.2. Damages

In (civil) labour cases, the losing party will, in principle, be sentenced to pay compensatory damages.

The amount of damages will generally be determined by law. However, in some limited cases, the employer and the employee can agree upon the scope of indemnification within the employment contract (e.g., a non-competition indemnity must, at least, be equal to half the gross remuneration corresponding to the duration of the non-competition clause, but the duration of the clause may – within certain limits – be agreed upon by the parties).

A penalty clause, where a party promises to pay a fixed sum if he/she fails to perform the contract or breaches a specific obligation, is rather exceptional in employment contracts and subject to Article 18 of the Employment Contracts Act, which stipulates that an employee can only be held liable for acts of fraud, a serious fault or a frequently occurring minor fault. An example is a penalty clause in case of a breach of confidentiality obligation after the termination of the employment contract. However, if the amount to be paid by the breaching party is obviously higher than the potential damages, which the parties could foresee at the time of entering into the contract, this clause will be null and void.

25.6.   Checklist of Dos and Don'ts

(1) Before initiating a legal procedure, consider the possibility to reach a settlement agreement out of the court (negotiations between the attorneys of both parties are confidential).
(2) Be sure to have sufficient evidence in order to prove your allegations. If this is not the case, try to negotiate a settlement agreement.
(3) Reduce the risk of litigation by the following best practices:
    (a) keep open lines of communication with the employees and let them – to the extent possible – participate in decisions that affect them;
    (b) invest in the social dialogue with the Works Council, the Health and Safety Committee, the Trade Union Delegation and the Unions to avoid collective labour disputes or to have them settled promptly;
    (c) draw up accurate and detailed employment policies, have them reviewed by an attorney and update them on a regular basis to be in line with the applicable legislation;
    (d) draft complete and precise contracts;
    (e) document shortcomings, build up a file with written evidence and implement evaluation procedures;
    (f) seek legal advice at an early stage of a conflict, or even before a problem arises; and
    (g) stay up-to-date with the applicable employment law.

26.   EMPLOYER RECORDKEEPING, DATA PROTECTION AND EMPLOYEE ACCESS TO PERSONNEL FILES AND RECORDS

26.1.   Overview

Employers must comply with data protection rules, particularly the GDPR, the Act of 3 December 2017 (installing the national Supervisory Authority) and the Act of 30 July 2018 (implementation and specification of the GDPR rules), during the performance of the employment contract, as well as before and during the recruitment process and after the contractual relationship has come to an end.

The general principles that must be respected are the following (Article 5 of the GDPR):

– Principle of lawfulness, fairness and transparency.
– Principle of purpose limitation.

- Principle of data minimization.
- Principle of accuracy.
- Principle of storage limitation.
- Principle of integrity and confidentiality.

26.2.   PERSONNEL FILES

Employers have not only the right but also the obligation to keep personnel files containing employees' personal data. There is no specific legislation stipulating what should be kept in personnel files and for how long. However, the privacy legislation stipulates that the employer may not retain personal data longer than necessary for the accomplishment of the purposes for which the data were collected and used. Moreover, the employer is responsible for personnel files and must therefore ensure that the data are adequately protected from loss and destruction. In this regard, the controller (the person responsible for the data processing) must adopt technical and organizational measures protecting personal data against accidental or unauthorized destruction, accidental loss or modification, access, and other unauthorized processing of personal data.

For data that must be kept in the mandatory social documents, the processing of the data can rely on the ground provided in Article 6, 1, c): it is necessary for compliance with a legal obligation. However, it is recommended to receive the consent of the employee for the processing of additional information which is not covered by a legal obligation, even when a part of the legal doctrine is of the opinion that an employee cannot freely give his consent in an employment relationship (therefore, consent is best given before signing the employment contract).

Subject to limited exceptions, some categories of data may not be processed, i.e., sensitive data (defined in Article 9 of the GDPR as personal data revealing racial or ethnic origin, political opinions, religious or philosophical beliefs, or Trade Union membership, and the processing of genetic data, biometric data for the purpose of uniquely identifying a natural person, data concerning health or data concerning a natural person's sex life or sexual orientation), and data specifically regulated (such as data generated for electronic communication needs or national registration numbers). The processing of sensitive data can be exceptionally allowed with the explicit written consent of the data subject (the employee), but this will only be allowed if there is a legitimate aim for the processing and the processing is proportional in light of this aim. In any case, the GDPR made it difficult for employers to process data relating to the health status of their employees (and visitors) during the corona crisis.

The GDPR provides a margin of manoeuvre for the Member States who can implement specific rules, including for the processing of special categories of personal data (sensitive data). The Act of 30 July 2018 specifies certain exceptions on the prohibition to process sensitive data and, *inter alia*, provides additional conditions for the processing of data concerning genetics, biometrics or health. The employer will have to provide a list of persons who have access to this data, and they will have to be bound by a duty of confidentiality.

26.3. CONFIDENTIALITY RULES

Besides the obligation to keep personnel files safe, the employer also has an obligation to ensure confidentiality with regard to the processing of employees' personal data. This obligation also applies to the subcontractors of the employer (e.g., the payroll administrator). The controller must ensure that the persons acting under his/her authority may only have access and use the data when needed to carry out their functions. Moreover, the employees must be duly informed about the legal provisions on the protection of personal data.

26.4. EMPLOYEE ACCESS

An (ex) employee must always have the possibility to request and obtain access to the content of his/her personal data, although the employer is relatively free to determine the modalities of this access, particularly with regard to the consultation of the file or the process for obtaining a copy. The Data Protection Authority is strict for an employer who refuses access to personal data.

26.4.1. Information Provided to the Individual Concerned

Article 12 of the GDPR provides rights to the individual concerned. A distinction is made between data that is obtained directly from the person concerned (Article 13) and data that is obtained from some other person or organization (Article 14).

In the first case, the controller must provide, among others, the following information to the data subject at the time of data collecting:

(a) the identity and the contact details of the controller and, where applicable, of the controller's representative;

(b) the contact details of the data protection officer, where applicable;

(c) the purposes of the processing for which the personal data are intended as well as the legal basis for the processing;

(d) the legitimate interests pursued by the controller or by a third party;

(e) the recipients or categories of recipients of the personal data, if any;

(f) where applicable, the fact that the controller intends to transfer personal data to a third country or international organization.

In the second case, the controller shall provide the same information:

(a) within a reasonable period after obtaining the personal data, but at the latest within one month;

(b) if the personal data are to be used for communication with the data subject, at the latest at the time of the first communication to that data subject; or

(c) if a disclosure to another recipient is envisaged, at the latest when the personal data are first disclosed.

The Act of 30 July 2018 provides for some exceptions for the right to information of the individual concerned, e.g., when the information directly or indirectly comes from the government services and the judicial authorities.

26.4.2. Right of Access and of Rectification

Article 15 of the GDPR establishes a right for the individual concerned to obtain from the controller confirmation as to whether or not personal data concerning him or her are being processed, and, where that is the case, access to the personal data and information such as the purposes of the processing, the categories of personal data concerned, the recipients or categories of recipient to whom the personal data have been or will be disclosed. In certain cases, the employer does not need to comply with the request to access, e.g., when there is a genuine risk that this would endanger the business secrets of the company or when complying with the request would demand a disproportional effort from the employer.

Article 16 of the GDPR provides the right for the individual concerned to obtain from the controller without undue delay the rectification of inaccurate personal data concerning him or her.

According to Article 17, the individual also has the right to obtain from the controller the erasure of personal data concerning him or her without undue delay where one of the grounds foreseen by the GDPR applies (e.g., when the personal data are no longer necessary in relation to the purposes for which they were collected or otherwise processed or when the personal data have been unlawfully processed).

The Act of 30 July 2018 provides exceptions, similar to the above-mentioned ones, for the rights in Articles 15–17 (e.g., exception for government data).

Should these provisions (Articles 15–17) not be observed, mediation could be led by the Data Protection Authority on the data subject's initiative (Article 62 of the Act of 3 December 2017). The Data Protection Authority also has a Dispute Resolution Chamber which can review a complaint and impose a fine. However, the Data Protection Authority cannot award damages to the victim of an unlawful data processing. Therefore, the data subject can also bring a court action before the President of the Court of First Instance in summary proceedings. The Data Protection Authority can refer a case to the Court of First Instance and become a party before that court. Finally, a Criminal Court procedure is also possible in case of a criminal offence referred by the Data Protection Authority to the Public Prosecutor.

The choice of the procedure will influence the outcome:

– Through the mediation procedure, various outcomes can be reached: access to data granted to the data subject, verification and possible erasure of personal data. If no amicable settlement is reached, the Data Protection Authority gives advice on the merits of the complaint, submits the litigation to the Court of First Instance, and/or informs the Public Prosecutor of any criminal offence.
– Through the dispute resolution procedure at the Dispute Resolution Chamber of the Data Protection Authority, the Act of 3 December 2017 provides for sixteen different outcomes, which include: to order the out-of-court settlement or to propose a settlement; to formulate warnings and reprimands; to order that the requests of the person concerned to exercise his rights be complied with; to order that processing be temporarily or permanently frozen, restricted or prohibited, to order that processing be brought into conformity; to impose penalty payments (to enforce the decision); to order the transfer of the file to the Public Prosecutor's Office of the Brussels Public Prosecutor, who will inform it of the action taken on the file. An appeal is possible before the so-called Market Court (special chamber within the Court of Appeal of Brussels).
– Through a civil court procedure, any person who has suffered material or non-material damage as a result of an infringement of the GDPR has the right to receive compensation from the controller or processor for the damage suffered (Article 82, § 1). The data subject has the right to mandate a not-for-profit body, organization or association to act on his/her behalf (Article 80).

– Finally, Criminal Courts can order the defendant to pay a fine of up to EUR 20 million, or in the case of an undertaking, up to 4% of the total worldwide annual turnover of the preceding financial year, whichever is higher (Article 83 of the GDPR). The court can also order an entire or partial publication of the judgment in one or more newspapers at the expense of the convicted person, a seizure of the media containing the personal data or an erasure of the data, a prohibition to manage any processing of personal data for a maximum of two years, and a financial compensation if the data subject filed a civil claim.

27.   REQUIRED NOTICES AND POSTINGS

27.1.   OVERVIEW

Belgian labour law requires employers to provide certain information to their employees by posting it in the undertaking.

27.1.1.   The Work Rules

In case of implementation or modification of the Work Rules, a specific procedure needs to be complied with. In the absence of a Works Council within the company, it is the responsibility of the employer to post a draft of the Work Rules or the proposed modifications to the Work Rules in order to give the employees the possibility to submit comments and suggestions for adaptations.

Furthermore, a copy of the Work Rules must be kept at each site where employees are employed. The employer must post a notice stating where the Work Rules can be found and consulted.

Every employee should, at any time and without the intervention of any other person, be able to access the Work Rules and its modifications in a place that is easily accessible.[36] A superior's office would not meet that requirement, as this would be a practical or psychological barrier that is difficult to cross for the employee.

The law explicitly states that notices should be 'posted', i.e., stuck to a wall in printed form. Publishing it on the intranet does not meet that requirement, but in practice, the Social Inspectorate generally tolerates this new form of posting, provided that every employee has free and easy access to these notices.

---

36. The Act itself does not contain the word 'easily'; however, it was clearly mentioned during the parliamentary discussions (Parl. St. *Senate* 1963–1964, 277, p. 5).

Finally, every employer is required to give a copy of the Work Rules to its employees. An e-document available on the intranet would also be acceptable as long as its access is free of additional cost and the authenticity of the document is guaranteed.

Failure to comply with all of these posting obligations can give rise to criminal liability.

27.1.2. Part-Time Work

A copy of all part-time employment contracts with an extract containing the applicable fixed work schedule (or the weekly duration of work with reference to the variable work schedules defined per the Work Rules) and the identity and signature of the employer and the employee must be kept at all times in the same spot as the Work Rules. The Social Inspectorate Services must be given access to these documents in order for them to verify compliance with all rules and regulations on part-time work. If part-time employees work on the basis of variable working time schedules, a written and dated notice regarding their daily working hours must be communicated to them, at the latest five days in advance (or less with a minimum of one working day beforehand if a CBA made compulsory by Royal Decree allows it), and kept within the company's premises at a spot where the employees have access to the Work Rules. The employer has to fill out all derogations from the applicable work schedule in a 'derogation register' (*afwijkingsregister – registre de dérogation*). This register must be kept in a spot that is easily accessible to the Social Inspectorate Services.

Failure to do so not only results in criminal liability but will also mean that the National Social Security Office can consider the employee to have been working full-time unless proven otherwise. As a result, the National Social Security Office will be entitled to claim social security contributions on the basis of full-time employment.

27.1.3. Miscellaneous

Every four years, social elections are organized in order to elect employee representatives for the Works Council and the Health and Safety Committee. During this election process, specific information needs to be posted at regular intervals. A billboard or any other means of official communication that allows for members of this Works Council and Health and Safety Committee to inform other employees of their activities must be provided for.

A decision to close the company must also be announced by a dated and duly signed document to be posted in a visible spot within the company premises.

Inspectors of the Social Inspectorate can enforce these obligations on the employer.

27.2.   CHECKLIST OF DOS AND DON'TS

– Install a billboard that is visible and accessible to all employees.
– Post draft Work Rules and all future modifications of the Work Rules.
– Post a notice of where the Work Rules are to be found and store them in a place that is easily accessible to all.
– Store signed copies of all individual part-time employment contracts containing the employees' work schedules in the same spot as the Work Rules.
– Communicate variable work schedules to part-time employees at least five working days in advance.

the employee's dress was in no way harmful to the employer. This was the case of a shoe shop assistant who converted to Islam during her occupation and started wearing long and loose-fitting tunics in dark colours. She was awarded a lump sum in compensation for moral damages incurred for being dismissed on the grounds of her religious beliefs.[33]

The dismissal of a hairdresser who persistently showed up in eccentric clothing and sporting long hair was not considered abusive as the employer was justified in wishing to maintain an elegant and classical style in his salon.[34]

21.2. CHECKLIST OF DOS AND DON'TS

– Provide clean work attire, free of charge, if the employee runs the risk of spoiling his/her clothes.
– Do not allow employees to take work attire home unless they work outside the company premises, and there is no health and safety risk to the employee or his/her family.
– Only impose a dress code if it is based on reasonable grounds, with a view towards achieving a legitimate goal and clearly set out the principles in a company policy that is accessible to all.
– Avoid future discussions by communicating clearly on dress standards.

22. PRIVACY, TECHNOLOGY AND TRANSFER OF PERSONAL DATA

22.1. PRIVACY RIGHTS OF EMPLOYEES

The right to privacy is a fundamental right enshrined in Article 22 of the Belgian Constitution and Article 8 of the ECHR. An employee's right to privacy encompasses his/her employment environment.

However, restrictions on the right to privacy are permitted if they:

– are prescribed by law (*principle of legality, including transparency*);
– pursue a legitimate aim (*principle of purpose*);
– are necessary and proportionate (*principle of proportionality*); and
– are relevant in an employment relationship (*principle of relevance*).

In the workplace, the collection of data may violate an employee's right to privacy. This is why the Belgian employment law has adopted several CBAs which legislate different ways of collecting employees' data, such as,

---

33. Labour Court of First Instance Charleroi, 26 Oct. 1992, *Chron. Dr. Soc.*, 1993, p. 84.
34. Labour Court of Appeal Brussels, 10 Jul. 1992, *Chron. Dr. Soc.*, 1993, p. 39.